macmillan education

2A

#InstaEnglish

@Emma Heyderman @Fiona Mauchline
@Patrick Howarth @Patricia Reilly @Olivia Johnston

#InstaEnglish Walkthrough

STUDENT'S BOOK

Your book is made up of a Starter unit, 8 regular units, plus Review and Life Skills activities. Each unit is divided into the sections introduced here. Check out how your book is structured so you can make the most of it!

Starter

This two-page unit provides strategic language for you to kick off your studies!

Opening

All units open with a visual treat that will trigger your first thoughts on the main subject. What pops into your head as soon as you look at it?

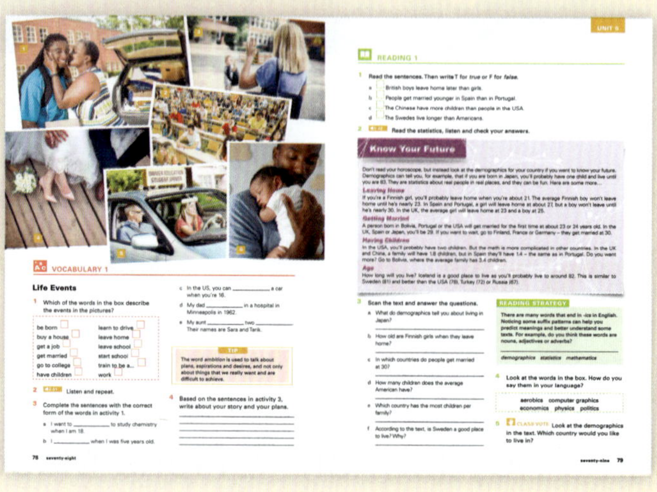

Vocabulary 1

Here you will read, listen to and look at pictures of words or phrases to begin exploring the unit topic. **Tip** boxes give you some advice to help make your learning easier.

Reading 1

Different text genres provide interesting content to practice your reading skills and introduce relevant language to be explored throughout the unit. The **Reading Strategy** box gives you tips on how to improve your reading.

Grammar 1

Grammar topics that were introduced in the reading text are systematically explored so you can easily work out all the rules and patterns. **Pronunciation** boxes help you master the tongue to speak more naturally.

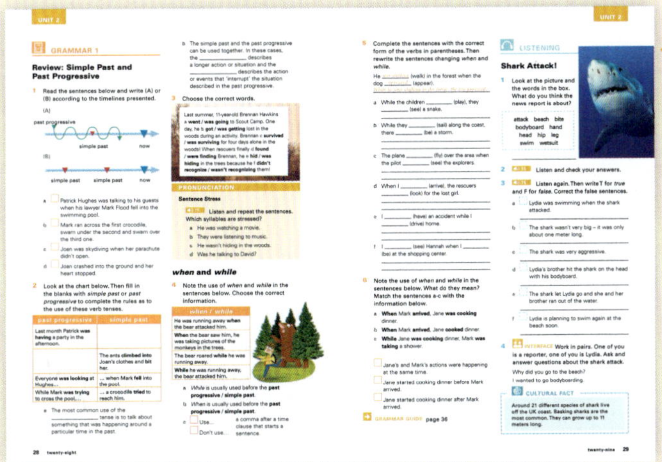

Listening

Learn and practice oral comprehension through engaging and contextualized oral texts. **Cultural Fact** boxes add little bits of cultural info to expand the topic.

Speaking

A clearly guided activity will help you practice your speaking skills using functional language in everyday situations.

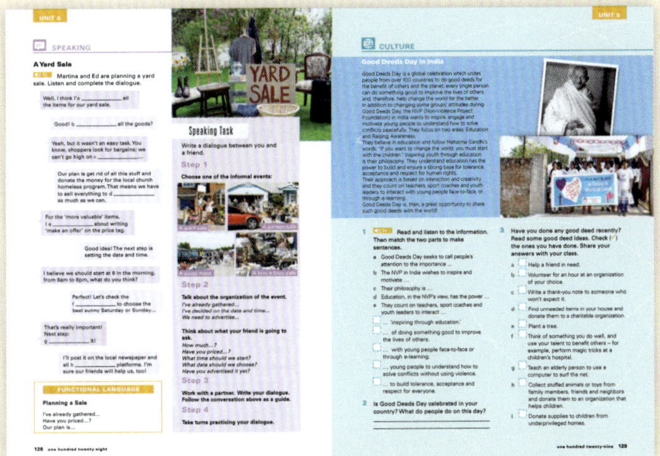

Culture

Discover cultural aspects of everyday life in countries around the world!

Vocabulary 2

The second vocabulary set provides more words and phrases to allow you to go further into the unit topic.

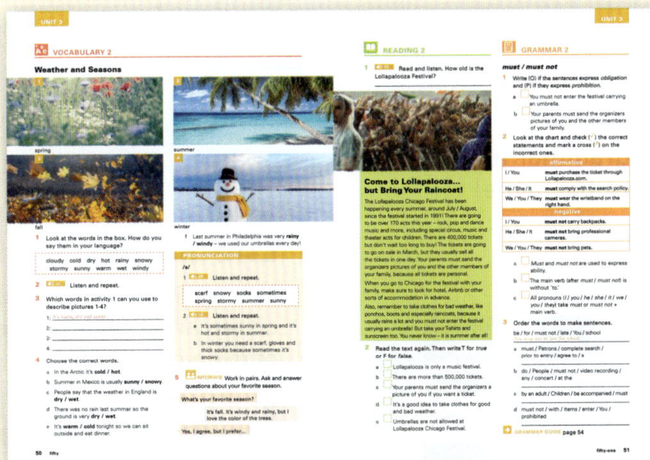

Grammar 2

This section introduces a new grammar topic in the same contextualized and systematized way that Grammar 1 does.

Reading 2

The second reading text digs further into the main topic and provides more language to be explored.

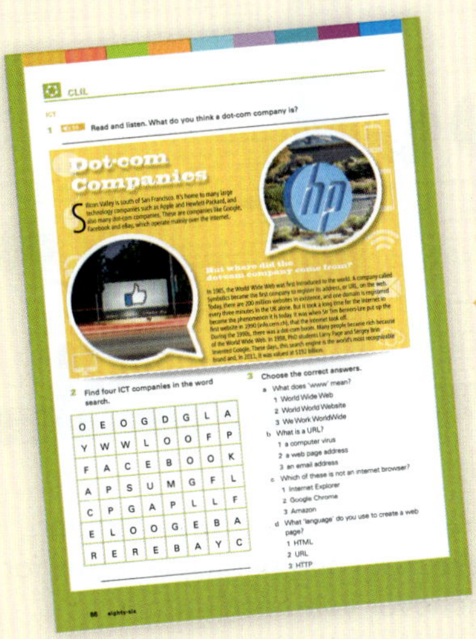

CLIL

Integrate your learning of the English language with other school subjects through fun texts and activities in every odd-numbered unit.

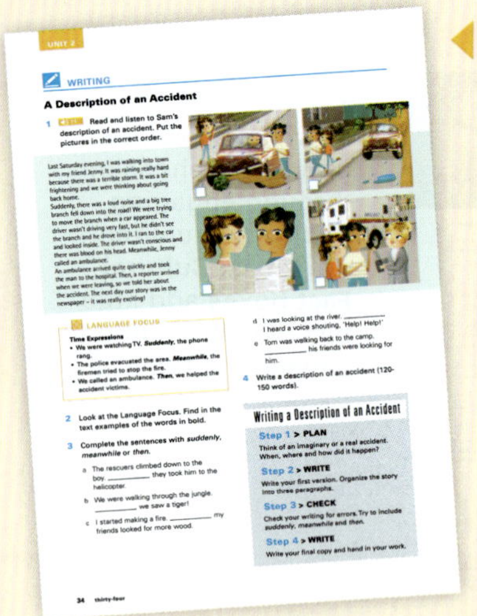

Writing

This section provides a model for the different text types you will get to practice in even-numbered units. The **Language Focus** box highlights useful language for written communication.

Vocabulary in Pictures

Have fun reviewing all the words and phrases learned in the **Vocabulary** sections, all richly illustrated!

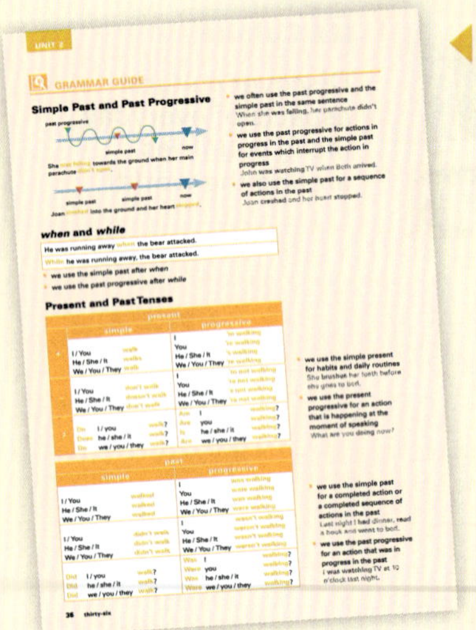

Grammar Guide

This is a reference section for all the grammar topics explored in the unit.

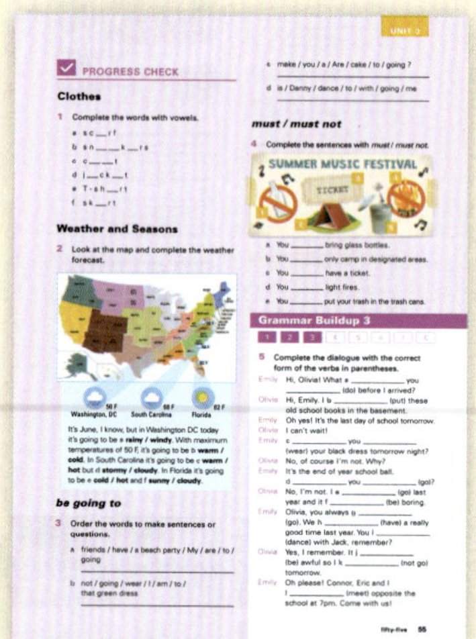

Progress Check

These activities help you revise core language and check your overall progress.

Reviews

Review the vocabulary and grammar from the previous two units starting with a game!

Life Skills

Learn skills to boost your talents, be a world citizen and deal effectively with the challenges of everyday life.

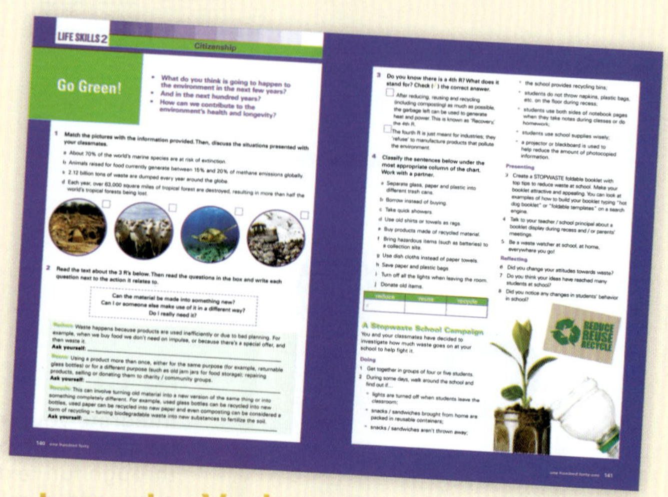

Irregular Verbs

A list with the most commonly used irregular verbs in their base, past and participle forms for you to check whenever you need them!

WORKBOOK

The workbook offers target-language practice and additional study material (consolidation and extension). It can be used as homework, independent study or extra classroom practice. Some of the sections correspond to sections in the Student's book:

Vocabulary 1

Grammar 1

Vocabulary 2

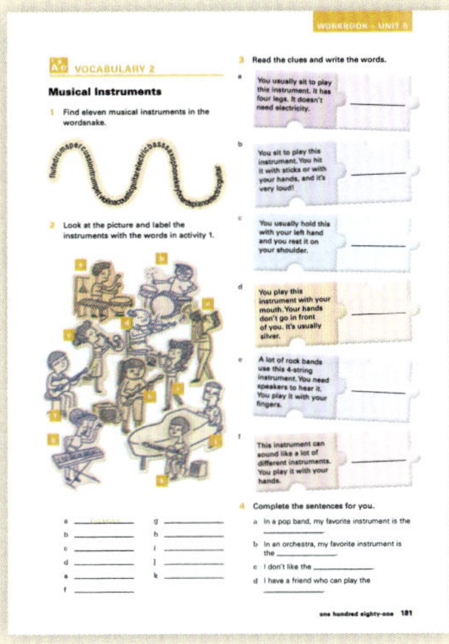

Grammar 2

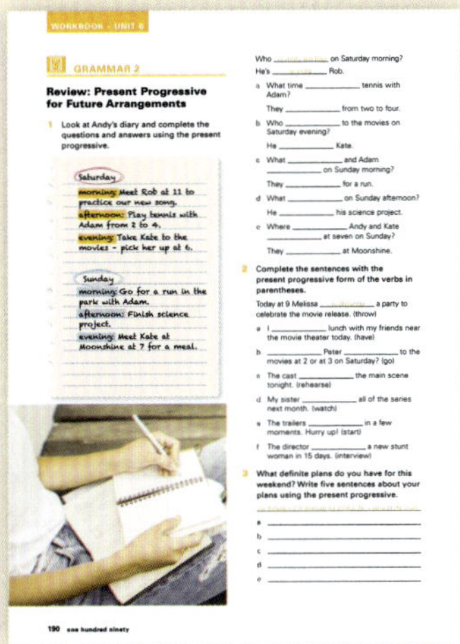

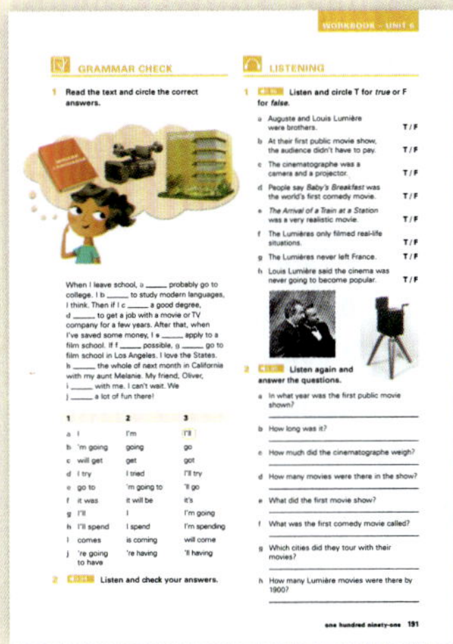

Grammar Check

A text with interesting, curious facts helps you check your reading and language skills.

Listening

Extension

This engaging section offers an extra challenge on grammar and vocabulary items.

Vocabulary Plus

Learn more words related to the unit topic in a fun way! All words are illustrated.

Wordlist

An alphabetical list of the key vocabulary in the **Student's Book** and from the **Vocabulary Plus** sections. It includes phonetic transcriptions and audio recordings.

DIGITAL STUDENT'S BOOK

This is the digital version of your **Student's Book** and **Workbook**, and you can easily access them everywhere! You will be able to read all the texts while having easy access to embedded audio tracks. Beside that, we also offer extra activities that can be monitored by your teacher so you can get the most out of your course!

CONTENTS

Starter

Free-time Activities

1 🔊 2 Listen to Megan, Dan and Rita talking about their hobbies and underline their favorite free-time activities.

- **a** Hi, I'm Megan. My hobbies are playing **the guitar / video games** and making models. This is my friend Dan.
- **b** Hello. I'm Dan. I like doing **volunteer work / karate** and going to the **gym / movies**.
- **c** Hi. I'm Rita. I love going **to the gym / out for a meal**. Luckily, I like going **to the gym / out for a meal**, too!
- **d** We all love **hanging out / relaxing / going to a youth group**. We always have a great time together.

Character Adjectives and Formation of Adverbs

2 Match adjectives a-h with their opposites.

a cautious	unsociable
b talkative	funny
c friendly	adventurous
d generous	lazy
e energetic	dishonest
f serious	confident
g shy	quiet
h honest	selfish

3 Complete the sentences with the adverb form of the adjectives in bold.

- **a** **Quiet**, please. Enter the library ___________.
- **b** Jennifer is a very **good** singer. She can sing really ___________.
- **c** Be **careful** with the dishes. Carry them ___________.
- **d** '**Fast** finishers' are students who finish their tasks ___________.

Rooms, Furniture and Gadgets

4 Cross the odd one out. Then add one more word to each group.

- **a** sofa, table, desk, camera, ___________________________.
- **b** dishwasher, fridge, lamp, stove, ___________________________.
- **c** toilet, electric toothbrush, microwave, mirror, ___________________________.
- **d** armchair, sofa, chair, wardrobe, ___________________________.
- **e** telephone, washing machine, laptop, TV, ___________________________.
- **f** cabinet, bathroom, bedroom, kitchen, ___________________________.
- **g** mouse, printer, speakers, bookcase, ___________________________.

Places to Visit

5 Find in the word spiral the name of twenty places to visit.

6 3 Listen, repeat and check your answers.

Comparatives and Superlatives

7 Choose the correct words.

- **a** Bikes are **better** / **the best** for the environment than cars.
- **b** What was **more interesting** / **the most interesting** book you read last year?
- **c** My brothers and sisters are **older** / **the oldest** than me.
- **d** That is **taller** / **the tallest** building in my town.

Simple Present and Present Progressive

8 Match questions a-d with the correct answers.

a	Do you have any questions?	No, he doesn't.
b	Are you having any difficulty with the task?	Yes, he is.
c	Does he usually write answers in pencil?	No, we're not.
d	Is he writing the answers in pen?	Yes, we do.

9 4 Listen and check your answers.

Simple Past and Past Progressive

10 Write questions.

- **a** have / Did / you / any / night / dreams / last ?
  ____
  ____
- **b** class / before / What / you / doing / this / were ?
  ____
  ____
- **c** yesterday / raining / Was / it?
  ____
  ____
- **d** last week / any / you / visit / Did / relatives ?
  ____
  ____

11 INTERFACE Work in pairs. Ask and answer the questions in activity 10.

Was it raining yesterday?

No, it wasn't.

1 Technology

20:16
20:16

VOCABULARY 1

IT Activities

1 Look at the picture. Can you name the equipment?

1 *games console* __________
2 __________
3 __________
4 __________
5 __________
6 __________
7 __________
8 __________
9 __________
10 __________

2 🔊 5 Check your answers and repeat.

3 What equipment do you use to do each of these things?

[*6, 7*] take a digital picture
a [ ] play a video game
b [ ] make a phone call
c [ ] scan a picture
d [ ] send an email
e [ ] store data
f [ ] go online
g [ ] print a document
h [ ] charge a cell phone/e-reader
i [ ] post a comment
j [ ] download / upload a song
k [ ] read an e-book
l [ ] plug in a memory stick

READING 1

1 Look at the text below. What genre does it illustrate?

a a blog post b a newspaper feature

A High-tech Bedroom

We took a peek inside a typical teenager's bedroom and what did we find? Well, we didn't find many books, but there were a lot of electronic gadgets. Student Ashley Judd, 13, tells us about the electronic stuff in her room.

SMART TV

'When I passed my exams my parents gave me a 21-inch smart TV for my bedroom. It's right in front of my bed so I can watch my favorite movies while I'm in bed.'

COMPUTERS

'I got my first desktop computer for my 10th birthday. It's quite old now, but I use it for school work. I also have a laptop where I store all my school work. I use a flash drive to save everything I need to take to school. And I have a portable hard drive which I use to transfer heavier files from one computer to another, as well as to save all my pictures.'

PRINTER

'My parents bought a new printer and they gave me their old one. The printing quality is garbage and the paper often gets stuck. But it has a scanner so I can scan my friend's school notes because they are much better than mine!'

GAMES

'I played a lot of video games on a console when I was younger and I keep them and my old PlayStation on my bookshelf. I don't buy many now, but sometimes I download games to play on the computer if the graphics aren't too heavy.'

PHONE

'I didn't have a cell phone until I was 12. It was a birthday present. Now I have a new one. I bought it with the money I earned from a summer job. I don't usually connect to the internet when I'm out because it's too expensive, but I use it for making calls, listening to offline music, playing games and taking pictures.'

GUITAR AND AMP

'I saved US$300 and bought a second-hand electric guitar and an amplifier last year. Some friends and I formed a band. We wrote some songs and uploaded them on the internet. We're planning to perform live at school next month.'

DIGITAL CAMERA

'I lost my digital camera last month. It had about 600 pictures on it. But a friend gave me his old one which I use whenever I want to take better pictures.'

2 Read the introduction. What is the text about?

a a favorite electronic gadget
b the electronic equipment in a bedroom
c the best electronic equipment

3 🔊 6 Read and listen. How many pieces of electronic equipment does Ashley have in her room?

____

4 Write T for *true* or F for *false*. Then correct the false sentences.

a ☐ Ashley never watches TV in bed.
____
b ☐ Ashley's laptop is newer than her desktop.
____
c ☐ Ashley doesn't play games now.
____
d ☐ She doesn't use the camera on her phone.
____
e ☐ She plays the drums in a band.
____
f ☐ She uses her friend's digital camera.
____

5 Find the words in the text and match them with their definitions.

a peek	☐ obstructed
b stuff	☐ computer pictures
c garbage	☐ things
d stuck	☐ bad quality
e graphics	☐ have a quick look

GRAMMAR 1

Review: Simple Past

1 Read the sentences below. Circle the irregular verbs and underline the regular verbs.

- **a** When I passed my exams, my parents gave me a 21-inch smart TV.
- **b** I played a lot of video games when I was younger. They were addictive!
- **c** I didn't have a cell phone until I was twelve.
- **d** Did your parents give you anything special on your birthday? Was it nice?

2 Look at the charts below. Then complete the sentences that follow it.

	***was* / *were* (Simple Past of *be*)**
+	I / He / She / It **was** great! We / You / They **were** twelve.
–	I / He / She / It **wasn't** popular. We / You / They **weren't** young.
?	**Was** I / he / she / it nice? **Were** we / you / they young?

	Simple Past	
	regular verbs	**irregular verbs**
+	I **passed** my exams.	They **gave** me a smart TV.
–	He **didn't play** computer games.	She **didn't have** a cell phone.
?	**Did** you **save** any money?	**Did** you **get** anything special on your birthday?

- **a** The past forms of the verb *be* are __________ for I / he / she / it and __________ for we / you / they.
- **b** *Was* / *wasn't* and *were* / *weren't* are used in affirmative, __________ and __________ sentences.
- **c** *-ed* or *-d* are usually added to the base form of regular verbs in the __________ form.
- **d** In questions and negative sentences, the auxiliary __________ is used to form the simple past tense.

3 Complete these questions with the simple past tense of the verbs in parentheses.

- **a** What __________ (be) early cell phones like?
- **b** What __________ Martin Cooper __________ (invent)?
- **c** __________ the portable phone __________ (need) to be powered through a car?
- **d** How long __________ it __________ (take) for it to be available to the public?
- **e** What __________ Motorola __________ (do)?
- **f** When __________ Apple __________ its first iPhone? (release)

4 Match the answers below with the questions in activity 3 and find out about the history of cell phones.

- ☐ He invented a portable hand-held phone.
- ☐ No, it didn't.
- ☐ It took ten years.
- ☐ In 2007.
- ☐ They were 'car phones' – two-way radios used by taxi drivers and emergency services.
- ☐ Motorola introduced the first public cell phone.

5 Complete the text with the simple past form of the verbs in parentheses.

The Worldwide Web

Thirty years ago, there a __________ (not be) a World Wide Web and there b __________ (not be) any social networking sites. By 1994, there c __________ (be) about a hundred important websites – today there are millions! The web d __________ (develop) when search engines such as Google e __________ (become) available and more people f __________ (get) high-speed broadband in their homes. Today, it is hard to imagine life without the web.

CULTURAL FACT

Top 3 countries with highest number of internet users:
1st - China (772,000,000)
2nd - India (462,124,989)
3rd - United States (312,322,257)

6 Ashley made a list of things to do yesterday. Look at the list and write sentences about what she did / didn't do.

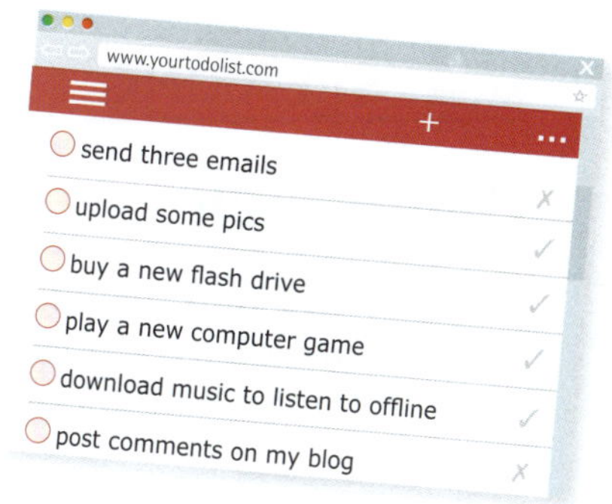

She didn't send three emails. ____________________

____________________ ____________________

____________________ ____________________

7 Read the spelling rules for the simple past of regular verbs. Complete the chart with the simple past of the verbs in the box.

download introduce play plug print scan store try

For most verbs, add *-ed*	
For verbs that end in *e*, add *-d*:	
For verbs that end in a consonant + *y*, preceded by a consonant, omit the *y* and add *-ied*:	
For verbs that end in a vowel + *y*, just add *-ed*:	
For verbs that end in a stressed vowel + a consonant (except *w*, *x* or *y*), double the final consonant and add *-ed*:	

8 INTERFACE Work in pairs. Ask and answer questions about last weekend. Use the ideas in the box or your own ideas.

download a song go online print a document send an email surf the web
take a digital picture upload a series use Instagram

Did you download a song last Saturday?

GRAMMAR GUIDE page 22

LISTENING

A Social Network

1 Read the sentences in activity 2 and check the meaning of any unknown words. Can you guess any of the answers?

2 🔊 7 Listen to an interview about social networking sites and choose the correct answers.

a … computer science students started Facebook.

1 Two 2 Three 3 Four

b Facebook became available to anyone over 13 years old in…

1 2004. 2 2005. 3 2006.

c Facebook is not permitted in…

1 schools.
2 some countries.
3 all offices.

d Facebook is … MySpace.

1 more popular than
2 not as popular as
3 as popular as

e The new verb 'unfriend' means…

1 to argue with a friend online.
2 to delete a friend from your friend list.
3 to find friends using your friends' list of friends.

SPEAKING

Online Tech

8 Rob and his dad Doug are surfing the net for Rob's birthday present. Listen and complete the dialogue.

Gee! Look at these **a** ________, dad! They look cool, don't they?

They really do.

Look, dad, wireless, great noise-cancelling tech and top-notch battery life!

I see, but they are expensive!!! So different from the ones sold when I was your age, in the 1980s.

What **b** ________ they like, dad?

Well, the 80s **c** ________ the Walkman era, so we **d** ________ small, portable and usually cheap headphones.

Walkman??? What was that?

It **e** ________ a small cassette player that **f** ________ in your pocket, but it was cool because people **g** ________ their own music tapes by mixing together songs that they **h** ________ off different albums.

So old! Nowadays we can download all our music from the internet!

Yeah, I know... well, let's get back to this new era, then. Which headphones do you want?

FUNCTIONAL LANGUAGE

Talking about Tech Gadgets

Look at this / these... They're cool!

What was it / were they like...?

Nowadays it is / they are...

Speaking Task

Write a dialogue between you and a family member (mom / dad / grandma / granddad).

Step 1

Decide which tech gadget you are going to talk about. Choose from the ones below or use your own ideas.

camera

cell phone

smartwatch

Step 2

Think about specific characteristics of the new gadget compared to a similar one from the past. If necessary, Google search some information about the old gadget.

Step 3

Work with your partner. Write your dialogue. Follow the conversation above as a guide.

Step 4

Take turns practicing your dialogue.

CULTURE

Singapore: Planning to Be the Next Tech Hub

Singapore, a city-state, is a multi-racial and multi-cultural island country with ethnic Indians, Chinese and Malays who are working hard to become Asia's next economic model. Under the leadership of its founder and 'Minister Mentor' Lee Kuan Yew, 45 year-old Singapore continues to be an icon of economic growth and political stability.

Singapore is identifying key sectors where it can join technology with the great market opportunities of Asia: biomedicine, clean-tech and digital media.

As to biomedicine, what Singapore has in mind is to focus on nano-medicine to try to detect cancer at its early stages, to offer computerized medical devices to help the recovery of stroke patients and provide the sustainable manufacturing of synthesized drugs. Singaporeans have an outstanding health service and the result is the lowest infant-mortality rate in the world and high life expectancy: 80 years of age for males and 85 for females.

Clean technology is also a target: water desalination, electric vehicles and hybrid buses are part of the project.

Artificial intelligence is also receiving investment.

Singapore is totally connected, globally aware and ready for more. Singaporeans are not afraid of taking strategic risks to reinvent their economy. The growth rate in this tiny city reached 18% – the highest in the world – making Singapore's dream come true.

1 9 **Read and listen. Then correct the sentences below.**

a Singapore used to be Asia's economic model, but it is not anymore.

____

____

b Singapore identified two strategic sectors where it can join technology with market opportunities in Asia.

____

____

c In biomedicine, Singaporeans just want to focus on nano-medicine to try to detect cancer at its early stages.

____

____

____

____

____

d Singaporeans have the highest infant-mortality rate in the world.

____

____

e Water desalination, electric vehicles and hybrid buses are part of the artificial intelligence project.

____

____

f Singaporeans don't like to take risks to reinvent their economy.

____

____

2 Can you list positive and negative impacts of technology on society?

____

____

3 Has technology influenced any sector in your country? Which sector(s)? How?

____

____

VOCABULARY 2

Jobs

1 🔊 10 Match pictures 1-6 with some of the jobs in the box. Then listen and repeat.

artist ☐ construction worker ☐
doctor ☐ fireman ☐ inspector ☐
journalist ☐ lawyer ☐
policewoman ☐ politician ☐
mailman ☐ researcher ☐
scientist ☐ technician ☐

1

2

3

4

5

6

2 Complete the sentences with jobs in activity 1.

a A __________ is someone who treats people who are ill.

b A __________ uses special equipment or machines.

c A __________ collects and delivers letters and packages.

d Picasso was an __________. He painted many pictures.

e A __________ collects information and does studies.

f A __________ has a job in politics.

3 Put the jobs in activity 1 into five groups. Add one or two more jobs to each group.

-man	-er
fireman	*lawyer*

-ist	-ian
journalist	*politician*

-or
doctor

READING 2

🔊 11 Read and listen to the article below. Answer the questions.

a What part of Martin's body did doctors implant in his eye? __________

b Do scientists think they can use the technology with other blind people? __________

A Miracle – Thanks to Technology

When most people think about new technology they think about a VR glass or a new cell phone – not Martin Jones. Martin was working as a construction worker when he had a terrible accident. Martin became blind because of the accident and for 12 years he couldn't see at all. Then doctors told him about a revolutionary new technology with a special optical lens that helps people see again. At first, scientists couldn't use the technology – they thought the patient's immune system might reject the plastic lens.
Then researchers discovered they could use the lens by implanting it in a different part of the body – in a tooth! Martin decided to try. Doctors took out one of his teeth, put the optical lens in it and implanted it into part of his eye.
Martin was blind when he met his wife, Gill. When he opened his eyes after the operation she was standing by his bed – she was the first person he saw. 'She's wonderful. It was unbelievable to see her for the first time,' said Martin. Now, he laughs about his 'science-fiction eye' and he's happy he isn't blind.
Scientists say the new technology can help more people in the future. They are already planning more operations.

GRAMMAR 2

Review: Past Progressive

1 Read the sentences. Underline the verbs in the past progressive and write (A) if the sentence is affirmative, (N) if it is negative or (Q) if it is a question.

a ☐ Martin was working as a construction worker.

b ☐ Martin's wife wasn't sitting by his side.

c ☐ Was Martin feeling good after the surgery?

d ☐ The doctors were developing a new technology.

e ☐ Were you reading anything about it?

2 Look at the chart. Then choose the best answer for the questions below.

affirmative	negative	interrogative
I / He / She / It **was working**.	He **wasn't working** when he fell off.	**Was** Martin **sleeping** when his wife arrived at the hospital?
We / You / They **were reading** about that new experiment.	They **weren't learning** about new technology.	**Were** you **surfing** the net when the lights went off?

a The past progressive is used:

☐ to talk about an action in progress.

☐ to talk about a completed action in the past.

b The past progressive is formed:

☐ with the main verb + *-d* (or *-ed*)

☐ with *was* for I / he / she / it and *were* for we / you / they + main verb *-ing* form

c The negative sentence is formed:

☐ by adding *not* to *was* or *were* (*was not – wasn't* / *were not – weren't*)

☐ by adding *didn't* before the main verb

d The question is formed:

☐ by adding *did* before the subject

☐ by placing *was* or *were* before the subject

3 What was happening when Beth got home? Complete the sentences with the past progressive form of the verbs in parentheses.

When Beth got home…

a her brother Mike ______________ (not write) an email, he ______________ (watch) TV.

b her parents ______________ (look) at a vacation website, they ______________ (not prepare) the meal.

c her sister Lisa ______________ (not listen) to music on Spotify, she ______________ (chat) online.

d her friend Jed ______________ (wait) for her, he ______________ (not use) the computer.

e the cats Sammy and Fifi ______________ (sleep), they ______________ (not eating).

4 Complete the text with the past progressive or simple past form of the verbs in parentheses.

Internet Helps Fight Crime!

Two weeks ago a robber took Dave Reed's laptop when he *was sleeping* (sleep). Dave's a writer and he **a** ______________ (write) a book at the time – it was all on the computer. Two days later, when Dave **b** ______________ (try) to find another computer on the internet he saw a laptop similar to his old one. Dave went to the seller's house to buy it. When he **c** ______________ (look) at the laptop, he realized it was his old one! When the man **d** ______________ (not look), Dave sent a message to the police. When the police arrived, Dave **e** ______________ (talk) to the man, but he **f** ______________ (not buy) the computer. The police found more of Dave's things when they **g** ______________ (search) the house. Dave got everything back – thanks to the internet!

5 INTERFACE Work in pairs. Ask and answer the question.

What were you doing at 8pm last night?

I was watching a Netflix movie.

GRAMMAR GUIDE page 22

CLIL

SCIENCE

Microwaves

Waves are vibrations that transfer energy from one place to another. Imagine a crowd doing the wave in a sports stadium. The people sit down, until it is their turn to stand up with their arms in the air, and then sit down again.
Like other electromagnetic waves, microwaves travel at the speed of light. Microwave ovens have a magnetron which produces these microwaves at a specific frequency.
The microwaves travel through the food in the oven, and the water molecules in the food start to vibrate. This vibration or movement of the molecules creates heat, which then heats the other molecules in the food.

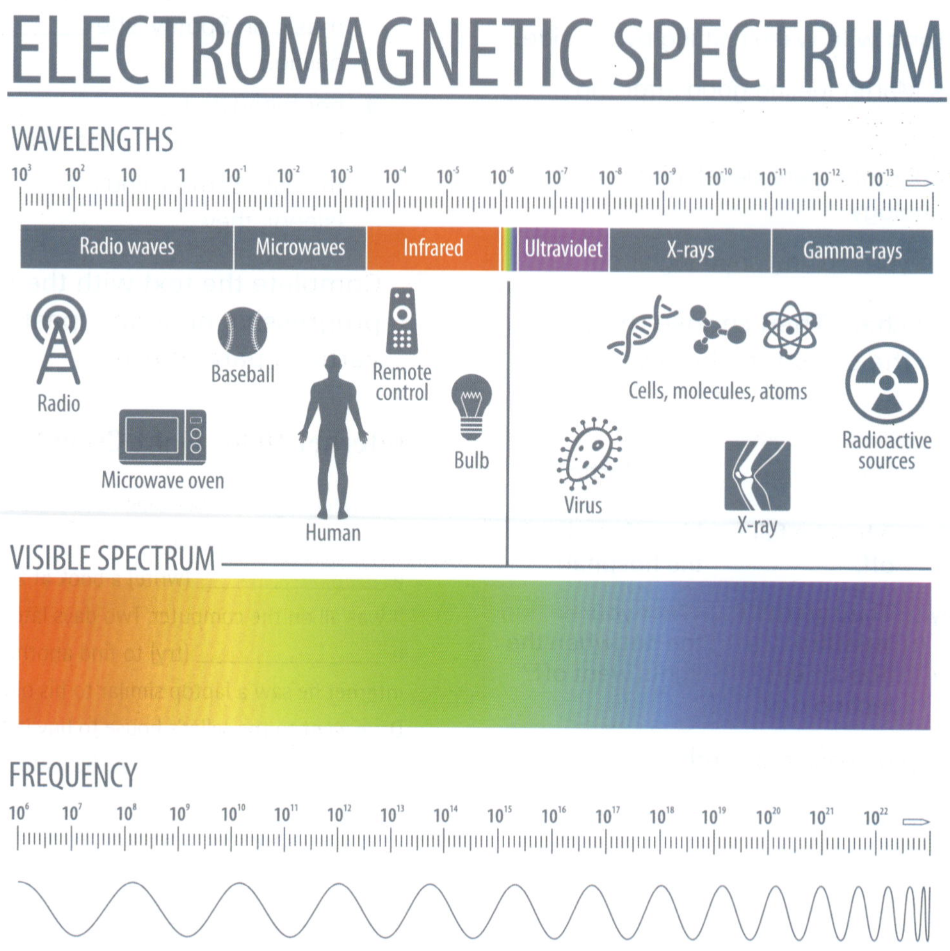

1 🔊 12 **Read and listen. Answer the question.**

Is it possible to cook dry food like rice or pasta in a microwave oven?

____

____

2 **Match the instructions to the labels on the diagram.**

a ☐ Microwaves make the water molecules vibrate.
b ☐ Microwaves travel through the wave guide to the food.
c ☐ A magnetron generates microwaves.

VOCABULARY IN PICTURES

IT Activities

charge a cell phone
download / upload a video clip
go online
make a phone call
store data
play a video game
plug in a flash drive
post a comment
scan a picture
take a digital picture
read an e-book
print a document
write a blog
send an email

Jobs

-er

construction worker
lawyer
researcher

-or

inspector
doctor

-man / -woman

fireman
mailman
policewoman

-ist

journalist
scientist
artist

-ian

politician
technician

GRAMMAR GUIDE

was / were

+	I	was	famous.
	You	were	
	He / She / It	was	
	We / You / They	were	

–	I	wasn't	famous.
	You	weren't	
	He / She / It	wasn't	
	We / You / They	weren't	

?	Was he / she / it famous? Yes, he was. No, he wasn't.
	Were we / you / they famous? Yes, we were. No, we weren't.

Spelling: Simple Past Regular Verbs

- for most verbs add *-ed*
  invent → invent*ed*
- for verbs that end in *e*, add *-d*
  arrive → arrive*d*
- for verbs that end in a consonant + *y*, omit the *y* and add *-ied*
  study → stud*ied*
- for verbs that end in stressed vowel + consonant, double the consonant
  scan → scan*ned* **refer → refer*red***

Spelling: Simple Past Irregular Verbs

- for the irregular verbs list, see page 142.

Simple Past

+	I / You / He / She / It We / You / They	scanned a photo.
–	I / You / He / She / It We / You / They	didn't scan a photo.

?	Did I / you / he / she / it scan a photo? Yes, I did. / No, I didn't.
	Did we / you / they scan a photo? Yes, we did. / No, we didn't.

- we use the simple past to talk about events in a definite time in the past

Past Progressive

+	I	was working.
	You	were working.
	He / She / It	was working.
	We / You / They	were working.

–	I	wasn't working.
	You	weren't working.
	He / She / It	wasn't working.
	We / You / They	weren't working.

?	Was he / she / it working? Yes, he was. No, he wasn't.
	Were we / you / they working? Yes, we were. No, we weren't.

- we use the past progressive to describe actions that were in progress in the past

PROGRESS CHECK

IT Activities

1 Complete the phrases with vowels.

a PL ___ Y ___ V ___ D ___ ___ G ___ M ___

b P ___ ST ___ C ___ M M ___ NT

c CH ___ RG ___ ___ C ___ L L PH ___ N ___

d G ___ ___ N L ___ N ___

Jobs

2 Complete the sentences with the correct jobs.

a Kathy is a ___________. She's investigating new technology at the moment.

b Joe works in construction. He's a ___________________.

c Sarah is a ___________, she works in a laboratory.

d Dalí is a famous ___________. I like his paintings.

Simple Past

3 Complete the sentences with the correct form of *be*.

a At 11pm last night Mark _________ in bed.

b Where _________ you at 7pm yesterday?

c They _________ at school yesterday because it _________ Sunday.

d I _________ at home last night because I _________ at my grandma's house. It _________ her birthday.

e _________ Kevin at the party last Saturday?

f No, he _________.

4 Look at Rita's list of things to do yesterday. Write questions.

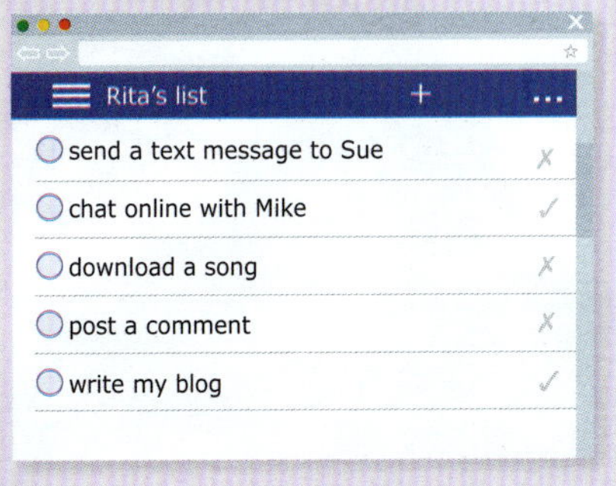

Did Rita send a text message to Sue?

a ______________________________

b ______________________________

c ______________________________

d ______________________________

5 Look at the list in activity 4 again and write answers to your questions.

No, she didn't.

a ______________ c ______________

b ______________ d ______________

Past Progressive

6 Write questions using the past progressive. Then answer the questions so they are true for you.

a what / you / do / at 10pm last night?

____

____

b what / your parents / do / at 3pm on Sunday?

____

____

c you and your friend / watch a movie / at 9pm yesterday?

____

____

Grammar Buildup 1

1 2 3 4 5 6 7 8

7 Choose the correct words.

Cell phones are a relatively new invention. Before them, there a **was / were** two-way radios in taxis, police cars and ambulances, but users b **can't / couldn't** connect to the phone network. In 1910, Lars Ericsson c **installed / was installing** a phone in his car. He d **stopped / was stopping** at different places while he e **traveled / was traveling** across the country. Then he f **connected / was connecting** his phone to the national telephone network with long wires. The first real 'mobile' phone system g **started / was starting** in 1956 in Sweden. Today, people h **use / are using** cell phones every day.

2 Strange but True!

VOCABULARY 1

Prepositions

1 13 Listen and repeat the prepositions.

across	along	around	away from
down	into	out of	over
through	towards	under	up

2 Which prepositions are opposites? Write them in pairs.

under *over*

a towards ________ c up ________

b into ________ d across ________

3 Choose the correct words.

James Bond is always very active in his movies. He often jumps **a out of / towards** planes and parachutes **b over / down** to the ground, and then he runs **c up / under** mountains to the top, dives **d into / out of** rivers and then swims **e under / over** water to the other side. He jumps **f into / over** obstacles and moves **g towards / over** his objective. After that, he drives **h into / away from** his enemies in his Aston Martin car!

TIP

We can combine action verbs with different prepositions to indicate the direction of movement, e.g. *swim across, swim over, swim under.*

READING 1

1 Look at the words below. Do they relate to text A or B?

millionaire hospital ant dive

A ______________ B ______________

2 🔊 14 Read and listen to the following anecdotes in the blog posts. Check your answers.

A

Strange Stories February 13, 2019

Crocodiles in the Pool

Patrick Hughes is a millionaire. Last month, he was having a party and he took his guests on a tour of his mansion. In the garden he had an enormous swimming pool with four crocodiles.

'I don't know who to give my money to,' Hughes said. 'I want to give it to a brave person. Can anyone dive into the water, swim across the pool and climb out the other side? I'll give that person anything they want – my money, my house, anything!'

Everyone was looking at Hughes when suddenly there was a loud noise – somebody was in the pool! It was Hughes' lawyer, Mark Flood, an unpopular man. Everyone ran along the side of the pool as they watched Flood. He ran across the first crocodile, swam under the second and swam over the third one. He was desperately swimming away from the crocodiles. Finally, he climbed out of the pool just before the fourth crocodile could reach him.

'You are incredible!' said Hughes. 'Tell me, what do you want?'

'I want to know who pushed me into the pool!'

B

Strange Stories February 15, 2019

A Lucky Accident

Joan Murray loves adventure and she often goes skydiving. She doesn't normally have any problems, but one day disaster struck as Joan jumped out of the plane.

She was falling towards the ground at a speed of about 200 km per hour, when her main parachute didn't open.

At the last moment, her emergency parachute opened just 210 meters from the ground. Joan crashed into a field and her heart stopped. Luckily, she fell onto a mound of fire ants. The ants climbed into her clothes and bit her. Doctors believe the bites from the ants started her heart again. Joan was in the hospital for two weeks, but then she recovered completely. The accident didn't stop Joan – she started skydiving again a year later.

3 Read text A again. Then write T for *true* or F for *false*.

a ☐ Patrick Hughes told his lawyer to swim across the pool.
b ☐ The crocodiles didn't eat Mark Flood.
c ☐ Mark Flood chose to swim across the pool.

4 Read text B again and order the events.

a ☐ Joan's heart stopped.
b [1] Joan went skydiving.
c ☐ Joan went to the hospital and recovered.
d ☐ The fire ants bit Joan.
e ☐ Joan's parachute didn't open.
f ☐ Joan started skydiving again.
g ☐ Joan fell onto a mound of ants.

5 Find words a-d in the texts and then match them with definitions 1-4.

a ☐ struck — 1 was able to touch
b ☐ crashed into — 2 hit very hard
c ☐ recovered — 3 occurred
d ☐ reached — 4 got better after an accident or illness

6 CLASS VOTE Which story do you think is stranger? Which story is true?

GRAMMAR 1

Review: Simple Past and Past Progressive

1 Read the sentences below and write (A) or (B) according to the timelines presented.

(A)

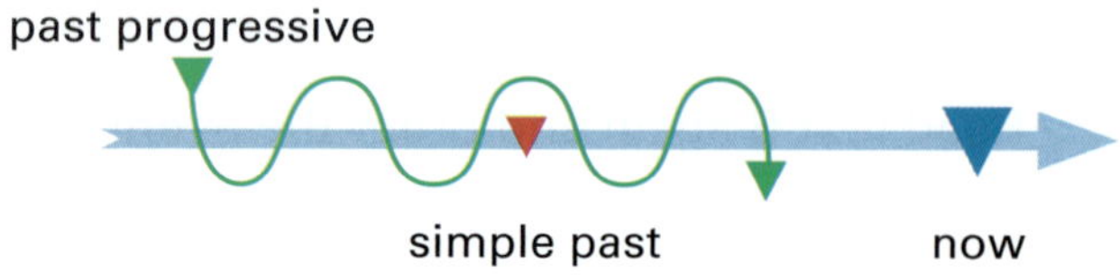

(B)

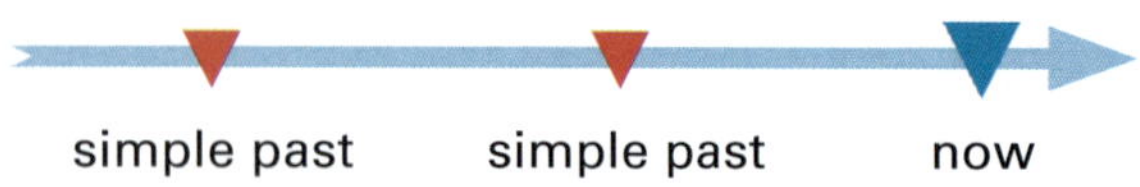

a ☐ Patrick Hughes was talking to his guests when his lawyer Mark Flood fell into the swimming pool.

b ☐ Mark ran across the first crocodile, swam under the second and swam over the third one.

c ☐ Joan was skydiving when her parachute didn't open.

d ☐ Joan crashed into the ground and her heart stopped.

2 Look at the chart below. Then fill in the blanks with *simple past* or *past progressive* to complete the rules as to the use of these verb tenses.

past progressive	simple past
Last month Patrick **was having** a party in the afternoon.	
	The ants **climbed into** Joan's clothes and **bit** her.
Everyone **was looking** at Hughes...	... when Mark **fell** into the pool.
While Mark **was trying** to cross the pool,...	... a crocodile **tried** to reach him.

a The most common use of the ________________ tense is to talk about something that was happening around a particular time in the past.

b The simple past and the past progressive can be used together. In these cases, the ________________ describes a longer action or situation and the ________________ describes the action or events that 'interrupt' the situation described in the past progressive.

3 Choose the correct words.

Last summer, 11-year-old Brennan Hawkins **a went / was going** to Scout Camp. One day, he **b got / was getting** lost in the woods during an activity. Brennan **c survived / was surviving** for four days alone in the woods! When rescuers finally **d found / were finding** Brennan, he **e hid / was hiding** in the trees because he **f didn't recognize / wasn't recognizing** them!

PRONUNCIATION

Sentence Stress

🔊 15 Listen and repeat the sentences. Which syllables are stressed?

a He was watching a movie.

b They were listening to music.

c He wasn't hiding in the woods.

d Was he talking to David?

when and *while*

4 Note the use of *when* and *while* in the sentences below. Choose the correct information.

when / while
He was running away **when** the bear attacked him.
When the bear saw him, he was taking pictures of the monkeys in the trees.
The bear roared **while** he was running away.
While he was running away, the bear attacked him.

a *While* is usually used before the **past progressive / simple past**.

b *When* is usually used before the **past progressive / simple past**.

c ☐ Use... ☐ Don't use... a comma after a time clause that starts a sentence.

5 Complete the sentences with the correct form of the verbs in parentheses. Then rewrite the sentences changing *when* and *while*.

He *was walking* (walk) in the forest when the dog *appeared* (appear).
While he was walking in the forest, the dog appeared.

a While the children ________ (play), they ________ (see) a snake.
____

b While they ________ (sail) along the coast, there ________ (be) a storm.
____
____

c The plane ________ (fly) over the area when the pilot ________ (see) the explorers.
____
____

d When I ________ (arrive), the rescuers ________ (look) for the lost girl.
____
____

e I ________ (have) an accident while I ________ (drive) home.
____
____

f I ________ (see) Hannah when I ________ (be) at the shopping center.
____
____

6 Note the use of *when* and *while* in the sentences below. What do they mean? Match the sentences a-c with the information below.

a **When** Mark **arrived**, Jane **was cooking** dinner.
b **When** Mark **arrived**, Jane **cooked** dinner.
c **While** Jane **was cooking** dinner, Mark **was taking** a shower.

☐ Jane's and Mark's actions were happening at the same time.
☐ Jane started cooking dinner before Mark arrived.
☐ Jane started cooking dinner after Mark arrived.

GRAMMAR GUIDE page 36

LISTENING

Shark Attack!

1 Look at the picture and the words in the box. What do you think the news report is about?

attack beach bite bodyboard hand head hip leg swim wetsuit

____

2 🔊 16 Listen and check your answers.

3 🔊 16 Listen again. Then write T for *true* and F for *false*. Correct the false sentences.

a ☐ Lydia was swimming when the shark attacked.
____

b ☐ The shark wasn't very big – it was only about one meter long.
____

c ☐ The shark was very aggressive.
____

d ☐ Lydia's brother hit the shark on the head with his bodyboard.
____

e ☐ The shark let Lydia go and she and her brother ran out of the water.
____

f ☐ Lydia is planning to swim again at the beach soon.
____

4 INTERFACE Work in pairs. One of you is a reporter, one of you is Lydia. Ask and answer questions about the shark attack.

Why did you go to the beach?
I wanted to go bodyboarding.

CULTURAL FACT

Around 21 different species of shark live off the UK coast. Basking sharks are the most common. They can grow up to 11 meters long.

SPEAKING

Zoo Story

17 Josh is talking to Mark about an event at a zoo near Chicago. Listen and complete the dialogue.

Mark, **a** __________ I **b** __________ you what I saw at the zoo last Saturday?

No. What happened?

Binti, the gorilla, **c** __________ a hero! She **d** __________ a little boy who fell into Binti's enclosure.

I don't believe it! You know, when animals feel they are in danger, they attack!

You bet! But, in this case, Binti **e** __________ the boy up gently and carried him to the door where paramedics **f** __________. I couldn't believe my eyes!

Really? How come?

In fact, when the boy fell he was unconscious. The keeper said she **g** __________ Binti to carry a doll and bring it to her, so Binti **h** __________ maternal instincts and probably **i** __________ the boy was the doll!

Lucky boy!

Yeah, but Binti's keeper insisted that Binti **j** __________ the boy; she was in no immediate danger and the other gorillas weren't around.

Fortunately, things **k** __________ out alright!

FUNCTIONAL LANGUAGE

Telling an Anecdote

Did I tell you...?
What happened?
Really? How come?

TIP

An anecdote is a short interesting or amusing story about a real incident or a person.

Speaking Task

Step 1

Think of an anecdote. Use the ideas below or your own ideas.

Step 2

Think about the specific details of the anecdote and how to tell it.

Did I tell you about...?
It was so frightening / interesting...
I was so embarrassed / bored...

Think about your friend's questions and reactions.

Really? How come?
What happened?
Where were you?
You were lucky / stupid / brave...

Step 3

Work with a partner. Write an anecdote. Follow the conversation above as a guide.

Step 4

Take turns practicing your dialogue.

CULTURE

Holy Animals of India

It may sound strange to Western civilization, but in India animals are considered sacred. This secular country strongly believes in the divinity of animals, especially those referred to in Indian mythology and ancient Indian culture.

The Cow

The cow is the holiest animal in India. It is treated as a god who has taken the form of an animal, a gift of the gods to the people. For that reason, slaughtering is banned all over the country. However, studies have shown that ancient Indians ate beef in ancient times. It was a myth, composed between 300 BC and AD 300, that led to the transition to not eating cows.

The Monkey

The monkey is considered to be a form of Hanuman – the god of power and strength. The biggest monkey, called Langur or Hanuman Langur, is the most sacred in India.

The Elephant

The elephant in India is part of Hindu culture. It is the god (divinity) of success and education. In the past it was used as an instrument of war. Nowadays, during festival seasons it is decorated and worshiped.

The Snake

Several old cultures worship serpents. The Indian Cobra is the most sacred snake in India and is revered by Hindus. Snake charmers are followers of Lord Shiva, the Hindu god who wears a king cobra around his neck.

The Royal Bengal Tiger

The Royal Bengal tiger, in all its strength and glory, is not only a sacred animal, but also the national symbol of India. Indians also worship the tiger because they are afraid of it.

1 🔊 18 **Read and listen to the text. Then write the animal the information below refers to.**

The Royal Bengal Tiger: It is the national symbol of India.

a ____________________: Its meat cannot be eaten.

b ____________________: It is revered by Hindus and the Hindu god, Lord Shiva, wears one around his neck.

c ____________________: It is the god of success and education.

d ____________________: It is the god of power and strength.

e ____________________: It was used as an instrument of war.

f ____________________: Indian people ate its meat in ancient times.

2 **Different animals mean different things in countries all over the world. Are any animals worshiped in your country?**

____

3 **How are animals (wild / farm / pets) treated in your country?**

____

____

VOCABULARY 2

-ed / *-ing* Adjectives

1 Look at the pictures and choose the correct word.

a The **couple** / **mountains** are frighten**ed**.

b The **couple** / **mountains** are frighten**ing**.

2 Complete the rules with *-ed* or *-ing*.

a We use ______ adjectives to describe how we feel.

b We use ______ adjectives to describe the thing or person that causes the feeling.

3 Complete the chart with the verbs in the box.

annoy bore excite frighten
interest surprise tire worry

verb	*-ing* form	*-ed* form
frighten	*frightening*	*frightened*

4 Choose the correct words.

a John is **bored** / **boring** because the movie is **bored** / **boring**.

b The results of the experiments are very **surprised** / **surprising**. The scientists are **worried** / **worrying**.

c I'm **annoyed** / **annoying** because my friend is late – again! It's very **annoyed** / **annoying** when people are always late.

d We're **tired** / **tiring** because it's very late, but the documentary is really **interested** / **interesting**.

e They are **frightened** / **frightening** of spiders. They think spiders are **frightened** / **frightening**.

5 19 Listen, check and repeat.

READING 2

1 Look at the pictures above and answer the questions.

a How do you think the people felt in the situation?

____

b What do you think happened?

____

2 Match words and phrases a-e with the definitions.

a get stuck ☐ care for

b look after ☐ come back

c return ☐ become trapped

d work ☐ be able to do something

e manage ☐ function

3 20 Read and listen to the news report. Answer the questions.

a What happened on the way home?

____

b Why didn't they use their phones?

____

c Who did they think about while they were trying to move the car?

____

d Who did they call on the way home?

____

e Are they planning to go again next year?

____

Mountain Couple Get Home Safely

Keith and Jennifer Lee live in Oregon, United States. Every year they go to the mountains. They don't usually have any problems, but last year things were different. They drove up to the mountains as usual, but as they were driving home they suddenly got stuck in the snow. Unfortunately, their phones weren't working so high up. It was a worrying situation.

While they were trying to move the car, they thought about their four children, aged 8 to 18. A friend, Sophie Smith, was looking after the children. When the Lees didn't return, Sophie became worried. She called the police and a search began.

Two days later Keith finally managed to move the car. They were driving home when they heard about the search for them on the radio. They were surprised! They called the police and then called Sophie. 'They're safe. They're coming home!' Sophie shouted when she heard the news. Everyone was delighted.

Keith is planning to go back to the mountains again next year, but Jennifer doesn't want to go. It was a frightening experience for her – she thinks they should stay in town!

GRAMMAR 2

Present and Past Tenses

1 Look at the chart below and match the sentences to the information below.

present and past tenses	
a	Every year Keith and Jennifer **go** to the mountains.
b	They**'re coming** home!
c	They **were driving** home when they got stuck.
d	Keith finally **managed** to move the car.

☐ It describes a habit.

☐ It refers to an action in progress in the past.

☐ It describes something happening now.

☐ It describes a completed action in the past.

2 Refer to the chart in activity 1 and use the verb tenses in the box to complete the information below.

simple past   simple present
present progressive   past progressive

a It describes a habit: ____________

b It refers to an action in progress in the past: ____________

c It describes something happening now: ____________

d It describes a completed action in the past: ____________

3 Read the text *Mountain couple get home safely* again and provide suitable questions for these answers.

a Where ______________________?
Keith and Jennifer Lee live in Oregon, in the U.S.

b What ______________________?
They were driving home when they got stuck in the snow.

c ______________________?
No, their phones weren't working.

d Who ______________________?
Sophie did and the search began.

e ______________________
______________________?
No, only Keith is planning to go back to the mountains next year.

4 Complete the text with the correct form of the verbs in parentheses.

Vanessa Horrocks _was watching_ (watch) TV in her apartment when she a __________ (hear) a strange noise in the bathroom. She b __________ (go) to check. She c __________ (have) a terrible shock when she d __________ (see) a two-meter-long python in the toilet. 'The snake e __________ (try) to get out of the toilet,' she f __________ (tell) our reporter, 'so I g __________ (run) out of the bathroom because I certainly h __________ (not want) to try and catch it. Then I i __________ (call) Fred, our building manager. He j __________ (arrive) quite quickly. He k __________ (catch) the snake and l __________ (take) it away.'
Vanessa still m __________ (feel) nervous when she uses her bathroom. 'And I always n __________ (put) the toilet lid down now,' she said.
Building manager Fred Murray told us: 'Pet pythons sometimes o __________ (escape) and p __________ (live) in the water systems of large apartment blocks. We q __________ (look for) the python's owner now. At the moment it r __________ (live) in a cage in my apartment but it __________ (grow) very fast.'

GRAMMAR GUIDE page 36

WRITING

A Description of an Accident

1 🔊 21 Read and listen to Sam's description of an accident. Put the pictures in the correct order.

Last Saturday evening, I was walking into town with my friend Jenny. It was raining really hard because there was a terrible storm. It was a bit frightening and we were thinking about going back home.
Suddenly, there was a loud noise and a big tree branch fell down into the road! We were trying to move the branch when a car appeared. The driver wasn't driving very fast, but he didn't see the branch and he drove into it. I ran to the car and looked inside. The driver wasn't conscious and there was blood on his head. Meanwhile, Jenny called an ambulance.
An ambulance arrived quite quickly and took the man to the hospital. Then, a reporter arrived when we were leaving, so we told her about the accident. The next day our story was in the newspaper – it was really exciting!

LANGUAGE FOCUS

Time Expressions

- We were watching TV. ***Suddenly***, the phone rang.
- The police evacuated the area. ***Meanwhile***, the firemen tried to stop the fire.
- We called an ambulance. ***Then***, we helped the accident victims.

2 Look at the Language Focus. Find in the text examples of the words in bold.

3 Complete the sentences with *suddenly*, *meanwhile* or *then*.

a The rescuers climbed down to the boy. __________, they took him to the helicopter.

b We were walking through the jungle. __________, we saw a tiger!

c I started making a fire. __________, my friends looked for more wood.

d I was looking at the river. __________, I heard a voice shouting, 'Help! Help!'

e Tom was walking back to the camp. __________, his friends were looking for him.

4 Write a description of an accident (120-150 words).

Writing a Description of an Accident

Step 1 > PLAN

Think of an imaginary or a real accident. When, where and how did it happen?

Step 2 > WRITE

Write your first version. Organize the story into three paragraphs.

Step 3 > CHECK

Check your writing for errors. Try to include *suddenly, meanwhile* and *then.*

Step 4 > WRITE

Write your final copy and hand in your work.

VOCABULARY IN PICTURES

Prepositions

down

out of

up

around

under

through

away from

across

over

into

towards

along

-ed / *-ing* Adjectives

annoyed / annoying

frightened / frightening

bored / boring

tired / tiring

excited / exciting

worried / worrying

surprised / surprising

interested / interesting

GRAMMAR GUIDE

Simple Past and Past Progressive

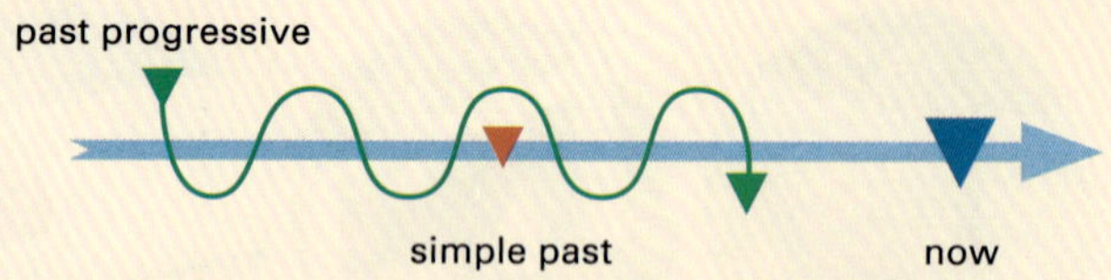

She **was falling** towards the ground when her main parachute **didn't open**.

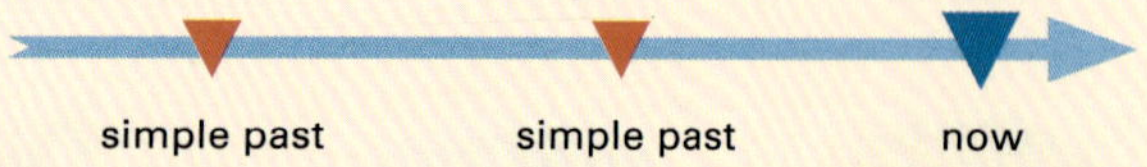

Joan **crashed** into the ground and her heart **stopped**.

- we often use the past progressive and the simple past in the same sentence
  When she **was falling**, her parachute **didn't open**.
- we use the past progressive for actions in progress in the past and the simple past for events which interrupt the action in progress
  John **was watching** TV when Beth **arrived**.
- we also use the simple past for a sequence of actions in the past
  Joan **crashed** and her heart **stopped**.

when and *while*

He was running away **when** the bear attacked.
While he was running away, the bear attacked.

- we use the simple past after *when*
- we use the past progressive after *while*

Present and Past Tenses

present	simple		progressive	
+	I / You He / She / It We / You / They	walk walks walk	I You He / She / It We / You / They	'm walking 're walking 's walking 're walking
–	I / You He / She / It We / You / They	don't walk doesn't walk don't walk	I You He / She / It We / You / They	'm not walking 're not walking 's not walking 're not walking
?	Do I / you walk? Does he / she / it walk? Do we / you / they walk?		Am I walking? Are you walking? Is he / she / it walking? Are we / you / they walking?	

- we use the simple present for habits and daily routines
  She **brushes** her teeth before she goes to bed.
- we use the present progressive for an action that is happening at the moment of speaking
  What **are** you **doing** now?

past	simple		progressive	
+	I / You He / She / It We / You / They	walked walked walked	I You He / She / It We / You / They	was walking were walking was walking were walking
–	I / You He / She / It We / You / They	didn't walk didn't walk didn't walk	I You He / She / It We / You / They	wasn't walking weren't walking wasn't walking weren't walking
?	Did I / you walk? Did he / she / it walk? Did we / you / they walk?		Was I walking? Were you walking? Was he / she / it walking? Were we / you / they walking?	

- we use the simple past for a completed action or a completed sequence of actions in the past
  Last night I **had** dinner, **read** a book and **went** to bed.
- we use the past progressive for an action that was in progress in the past
  I **was watching** TV at 10 o'clock last night.

PROGRESS CHECK

Prepositions

1 Complete the sentences with the words in the box.

across into out of under up

a When John woke up, he climbed __________ his tent and ate breakfast.

b Then he walked to the river and dove __________ the water.

c While he was swimming __________ the river to the other side, it started to rain.

d When he reached the other side, he sheltered __________ a tree.

e When the rain stopped, he ran __________ a big hill.

-ed / -ing Adjectives

2 Complete the sentences with the correct form of the words in parentheses.

a They are very late. I am ________ (worry).

b The movie was really ________ (bore).

c Were you ________ (surprise) when you saw me?

d I'm reading a really ________ (interest) book.

e I can't find my smartphone. It's really ________ (annoy).

Review: Simple Past and Past Progressive

3 Complete the sentences with the correct form of the verbs in parentheses. Use the simple past or the past progressive.

a John __________ (not get up) early yesterday.

b At six o'clock yesterday I __________ (do) my homework.

c They __________ (not do) anything when I __________ (see) them.

d Kate __________ (meet) Kevin while she __________ (walk) to school.

4 Complete the questions using the simple past or the past progressive form of the verbs in parentheses.

a __________ (you / go) to a party last Saturday?

b What __________ (you / do) at 3am this morning?

c What ____________________ (you / do) last night?

d What ____________________ (your mother / do) when you __________ (wake up) this morning?

e What ____________________ (the other students / do) when your teacher ____________________ (arrive) today?

Present and Past Tenses

5 Write sentences using the simple present, present progressive, simple past or past progressive.

a Nicky / watch a DVD / when / her friend / arrive.

____

b I / look for my friends / now.

____

c They / not usually eat / meat.

____

d While / they / swim / they / see a shark.

____

Grammar Buildup 2

1 2 3 4 5 6 7 8

6 Choose the correct words.

Todd Endris a **works** / **is working** in a laboratory, but he usually b **goes** / **is going** surfing in his free time. He loves c **surfing** / **surfed**! One day last summer while he d **is surfing** / **was surfing** at Marina Beach, an enormous white shark e **attacked** / **was attacking** him. Todd f **hit** / **was hitting** the shark on the nose, but it g **didn't release** / **wasn't releasing** him. He h **got** / **was getting** desperate when suddenly six dolphins attacked the shark and Todd escaped. Two other surfers helped Todd to the beach and i **call** / **called** an ambulance. Todd j **was** / **were** in the hospital for a long time, but he recovered. After a shark attack, most people are k **frightening** / **frightened** of surfing again, but not Todd. What l **does he do** / **is he doing** at the moment? Surfing, of course!

Review 1

VOCABULARY | GRAMMAR

Start

1

He's an amazing **artist** / **lawyer**!

2

The train went **around** / **through** the tunnel.

8

They're walking **round** / **along** the seashore.

7

He's running **outside** / **towards** the bus with a cup of coffee in his hands!

9

I often **charge** / **use** my cell phone in the car.

10

He's the **mailman** / **fireman** who brings all the correspondence to the neighborhood.

16

Although the news from the hospital is very **worrying** / **worried**, I know he's going to recover soon.

15

I'm **boring** / **bored**. Let's go to the movies.

17

I trust him to do this job in the house because he's an excellent **doctor** / **construction worker**.

18

The vehicles are going **up** / **round** the traffic circle.

3

My sister's very **annoying / annoyed**! She broke my printer last night.

4

I'm reading a book about the Arctic. It's really **interesting / interested**.

6

Sorry, I need to **make / do** a phone call.

5

Can I borrow your **laptop / flash drive** to save this document?

11

They're getting **out of / into** the plane.

12

I didn't like the movie. It was very **frightening / frightened**.

14

His shelves were filled up with books, so now he only reads **e-books / emails**.

13

I'm **tiring / tired**. I think I'm going to bed.

19

She's the **lawyer / engineer** who is taking care of our court case.

20

I prefer to **store / hold** data in the cloud so I can access it anywhere.

Finish

Review 1

VOCABULARY

GRAMMAR

Simple Past

1 Complete with *was(n't)* or *were(n't)*.

It __*was*__ my parents' 25th wedding anniversary yesterday. My mom **a** ________ excited; it was just another normal day. There **b** ________ many letters in the mail that morning, but there **c** ________ a card from my dad. When my mom opened it, there **d** ________ two airline tickets to New York in it. **e** ________ she excited then? Yes, she **f** ________. *Very* excited!

2 Complete the sentences with the simple past form of the verbs in parentheses.

I __*sent*__ (send) you an email last night.

a Marc ______ (take) a picture with his cell phone.

b He finally ______ (read) my blog!

c My mom ______ (work) at the school.

d I ______ (do) my homework after lunch.

3 Rewrite the sentences using the negative.

You charged your cell phone.
You didn't charge your cell phone.

a They scanned the document.
____

b I wrote a letter to the politician.
____

c He met Elena online.
____

d The computer stored the data.
____

4 Complete the simple past questions with the verbs in the box. Then write the correct short answers.

make	~~send~~	take	want	work

__*Did*__ he __*send*__ ten emails yesterday?
✗ __*No, he didn't.*__

a ________ you ________ to be an actor?
✓ ________________________

b ________ they ________ any pictures?
✓ ________________________

c ________ your sister ________ as an artist?
✗ ________________________

Past Progressive

5 Complete the sentences with the past progressive form of the verbs in parentheses.

I __*was*__ __*choosing*__ (choose) a new book in the library yesterday morning.

a A school boy ________ ________ (use) a computer near me.

b He ________ ________ (not do) his homework on the computer.

c He ________ ________ (play) a game.

d A man ________ ________ (wait) to use the scanner.

6 Write questions in the past progressive. Then underline the correct words in the short answers.

you / live / in Paris / last year?
Were you living in Paris last year?
No, **I was** / **<u>wasn't</u>**.

a it / rain / at 6 o'clock?
____
Yes, **he** / **it** was.

b Simon and Jen / work / as researchers?
____
Yes, they **was** / **were**.

c the students / download / documents?
____
No, they **were** / **weren't**.

VOCABULARY

GRAMMAR

Simple Past and Past Progressive

7 Underline the correct words.

I saw the accident while I **walked** / **was walking** to school.

- **a** A bus was coming along the road when a dog **ran** / **was running** in front of it.
- **b** The driver **saw** / **was seeing** the dog and tried to avoid it.
- **c** While the driver **tried** / **was trying** to avoid the dog, he drove into a tree.
- **d** I quickly got my cell phone and **called** / **was calling** the emergency services.

8 Complete the sentences with the correct form of the verbs in parentheses. Use the simple past or the past progressive.

Someone *went* into their room while they *were sleeping* (go / sleep).

- **a** While Lucas __________, he __________ his leg (ski / break).
- **b** I __________ home when I __________ a $50 bill (run / find).
- **c** We __________ when the teacher __________ in (chat / come).
- **d** Dad __________ a picture of us while we __________ (take / dive).

when and *while*

9 Complete the sentences with *when* or *while*.

I was surprised *when* I heard the news.

- **a** They saw dolphins ________ they were sailing.
- **b** We stayed inside ________ it was raining.
- **c** ________ he saw the bear, he was walking in the forest.
- **d** The dog was running towards me ________ it suddenly stopped.

Present and Past Tenses

10 Complete the sentences with the simple present or the present progressive form of the verbs.

My dad *gets* (get) emails every day.

- **a** We often __________ (go) out for a meal.
- **b** I __________ (make) a curry right now.
- **c** What __________ your mom __________ (do)?
- **d** She__________ (eat) an apple now.

11 Complete the text with the verbs in the box. Use the simple past or the past progressive.

~~do~~ play not know switch watch

I *was doing* my homework at 9 o'clock last night. I had to write a blog, but I **a** __________ what to write about. Then, I heard a noise outside. I **b** __________ off my light and looked out of the window. Three foxes **c** __________ in our garden. I **d** __________ them for ten minutes and then started writing my blog!

12 Number the sentences below according to the list of tenses.

1. simple present
2. present progressive
3. simple past (completed action)
4. simple past (sequence of actions)
5. past progressive (action in progress)
6. simple past and past progressive

[*3*] I slept badly last night.

- **a** [ ] We were sleeping at 11 o'clock.
- **b** [ ] Shhh! The baby's sleeping.
- **c** [ ] The phone rang while I was sleeping.
- **d** [ ] I sleep 8 hours a night.
- **e** [ ] I got into bed and went to sleep.

3 Celebrate!

VOCABULARY 1

Clothes and Accessories

1 Look at the words in the box. How do you say them in your language?

boots coat dress jacket jeans pants scarf shirt shorts skirt sneakers sweater T-shirt

2 22 Listen and repeat.

3 Match descriptions a-f to pictures 1-6.

a I'm wearing a pair of jeans and a brown coat. I'm having fun with my friends. ☐

b This is my uncle and his wife at their wedding. My uncle is wearing a special Scottish skirt called kilt. ☐

c This is me on the beach. I'm wearing a pair of shorts and a T-shirt. ☐

d This is New Year's Eve. It's December so we're wearing a coat, gloves and a scarf. ☐

e This is my little brother's birthday party. He's wearing a multi-colored shirt. ☐

f It's Thanksgiving Day and my mom's wearing her favorite sweater. ☐

TIP

We often use *a pair of...* with clothes: *a pair of pants, a pair of boots*. Remember that pants and boots are plural.
These are my favorite pants. ✓

4 23 Listen to Emily and Ben. What do they usually wear on special occasions?

____

____

____

____

5 INTERFACE Work in pairs. Ask and answer questions about the clothes you wear. Use the words in the box or your own ideas.

a party a wedding school New Year's Eve the weekend

What do you usually wear to parties?

I usually wear a pair of jeans and a black T-shirt.

READING 1

1 Skim the text and complete the headings with the words below.

a Gloves b Skirts c White

2 What genre does it illustrate?

a essay b feature article

Dress Properly for these Celebrations!

Men in ____________________

If you're going to go to a *ceilidh*, you're going to need your dance clothes and comfortable shoes. *Ceilidhs* are traditional dances from Scotland and Ireland, and the music is fast and energetic. Everybody dances and has a good time, and *ceilidhs* are as popular as nightclubs. Girls wear what they want: jeans, skirts or pants; boys wear kilts, shirts and jackets. A kilt is similar to a skirt – it is a traditional Scottish outfit and it's perfect for dancing!

Not All Brides Wear ____________________

When Indian women get married, the traditional color isn't white, it's red, because this color is the symbol of new life. So, an Indian bride doesn't wear a white wedding dress, she wears a beautiful, long, red *sari* with red and gold jewelry and red henna on her hands.

Good Fun in ____________________

You can be sure it is going to be cold on New Year's Eve at Times Square, NY, so wear warm clothes! Coats, scarves and boots are best. New Year's Eve has been celebrated at Times Square since 1904. Around one million locals and tourists gather near the New York Times' building to see a huge crystal ball descend from a tower during the countdown to midnight. And no one seems to complain about the freezing weather they have to endure to take part in this celebration. The organizers recommend many layers of clothing, a good hat, winter shoes and gloves. It's a magical night of lights, fireworks and friends, but anyone who doesn't dress warmly is going to freeze!

3 24 Read and listen to the text and answer the questions.

a Where do *ceilidhs* come from?

____

b What do girls wear to a *ceilidh*?

____

c What is the traditional color at an Indian wedding? Why?

____

d Why does the text recommend coats, hats and scarves for New Year's Eve at Times Square?

____

e What do people gather to see?

____

READING STRATEGY

When you read a new word, read the context – the words around it – and try to guess the meaning.

4 Scan the text and underline words for these definitions.

a a traditional skirt from Scotland for men.

b a woman who is getting married.

c a red substance to color hair or skin.

d the counting backwards of numbers before an important event.

e colorful explosives, typical at celebrations.

5 CLASS VOTE Which is your favorite celebration?

GRAMMAR 1

be going to

1 Read these sentences. Underline the verb *be* and circle *going to* + *verb*.

a You are going to need your dance shoes.

b The music is going to be fast and energetic.

c The Indian bride isn't going to wear white.

d They are going to freeze on New Year's Eve.

e We aren't going to take part in the Irish dance.

2 Look at the rules as to the use of *be going to* and complete the chart below.

a The verb *be* in the simple present (am / is / are) is used before *going to*.

b *going to* is followed by a verb in the base form.

c The negative sentence is formed with the negative form of *be* (am not / isn't / aren't).

affirmative
I _______ going to wear a coat on New Year's Eve.
He / She / It is _______ be cold tonight.
You / We / They _______ going to take part in the dance next Saturday.
negative
I _______ going to be inside.
He / She / It _______ going to stop the dance.
You / We / They aren't going to _______ any songs.

3 Order the words to make sentences.

a are / to / have / the beach / on / We / going / a party

____

b I / to / wear / am / clothes / fancy / going / not

____

c be / The music / to / going / great / is

____

d is / going / not / It / to / a barbecue / be

____

e am / sandwiches / I / take / going / cake / and / to

____

f great time / You / to / have / are / going / a

____

TIP

Use time expressions with *be going to* to talk about future plans: *this August / weekend, next Tuesday / Christmas, on the weekend, tonight, tomorrow...*

4 Look at Sarah's calendar. Complete her plans with the time expressions in the box.

next Monday　on Wednesday
this Thursday　on Friday
on the weekend　tomorrow

a Sarah's going to go to the movies with her friends ______________.

b She's going to buy a new dress ______________.

c She's going to study math ______________.

d She's going to take her science exam ______________.

e She's going to go to the school ball ______________.

f She's going to study for the science exam ______________.

July		
Monday	8	school excursion – museum
Tuesday	9	Jack and Ellie – movies
Wednesday	10	study science
Thursday	11	science exam
Friday	12	buy new dress
Saturday	13	summer barbecue – Youth Club
Sunday	14	study math
Monday	15	last exam – math! end-of-school ball

5 Look at the sentences below. Circle the verb *be*.

a Are you going to wear a kilt? No, you aren't.

b Is it going to freeze during the night? Yes, it is.

c Are we going to enjoy the night? Yes, we are.

d Am I going to have a great time? Yes, I am.

6 Complete the chart. Note the use of *be going to* in questions and short answers.

questions and short answers	
_______ I going to have a great time?	Yes, I am. / No, I _______.
_______ you going to wear a kilt?	Yes, you _______. / No, you aren't.
_______ it going to be a cold night?	Yes, it _______. / No, it _______.
_______ he / she going to bring a friend?	Yes, he / she is. / No, he / she _______.
_______ we / you / they going to be tired?	Yes, we / you / they _______. / No, we / you / they _______.

7 Look at the sentences in the chart in activity 6 again. What is the correct order for questions?

a subject + be + going to + verb + other words?

b be + subject + going to + verb + other words?

8 Write questions using *be going to*.

Who / Sarah / go to the movies with?

Who is Sarah going to go to the movies with?

a What / she / study on Wednesday?

____

b What / she / buy this week?

____

c What / she / visit today?

____

d When / she / take / her last exam?

____

e Where / they / have a barbecue?

____

9 Answer the questions in activity 8. Use Sarah's calendar in activity 4.

She's going to go to the movies with Jack and Ellie.

a _______________

b _______________

c _______________

d _______________

e _______________

10 INTERFACE Work in pairs. Ask and answer questions about your week.

What are you going to do on Saturday?

I'm going to play tennis with Jorge.

GRAMMAR GUIDE page 54

LISTENING

Costume Party

1 25 Listen to Emma, Ethan and Conor talking about a costume party. Match the names to pictures 1-3.

2

____

1

____

3

____

2 25 Listen again and choose the correct words.

a The party is on **Friday / Saturday**.

b Emma **is / isn't** going to take her straw broom.

c The party **is / isn't** going to be at Ethan's house.

d Ethan's parrot **is / isn't** going to be real.

e Conor is going to wear his **black / brown** boots.

f Conor **is / isn't** going to wear a scarf.

CULTURAL FACT

Costume parties became popular in the US in the 19th century. Rich people dressed like historic European aristocrats and wore original accessories as a way to show off their wealth.

SPEAKING

A Birthday Party

26 Lisa is making a WhatsApp call to Emma to invite her to her birthday party. Listen and complete the dialogue.

Hi, Emma! How are you doing?

Just fine, and you?

Great! In fact, I a ______________ a birthday party next Saturday. Do you want to come?

Cool! What time b ______________?

Well, I'm having a barbecue, so I think 1 p.m. is fine.

c ________________ all our friends from school?

Not all of them, I guess, 'cause I can't spend too much money on it... But Jade and Josh d ________________ ... if that's what you wanted to know...

Yeah, you know me quite well. Do you need help with anything?

No, thanks! My parents e ________________ everything!

Well, Lisa, see you on Saturday, then... oh, no, see you tomorrow at school!

FUNCTIONAL LANGUAGE

Extending and Accepting Invitations

I'm having...
I'm going to throw / give a... party...
Do you want to come?
Cool!
What time is it going to be?

Speaking Task

Write a dialogue between you and a friend.

Step 1

Imagine it is your birthday and you are having a party. First, choose the type of party. You can use the ideas below or your own.

Step 2

Decide what to say.

I'm going to throw a... on...
Do you want to come? / Would you like to come?
I'm going to invite...
It is going to start at...

Think about what your friend is going to say.

Cool!
Thank you!
I'd love to!
What time is it going to start?
Who are you going to invite?
See you...

Step 3

Work with a partner. Write your dialogue. Follow the conversation above as a guide.

Step 4

Take turns practicing your dialogue.

CULTURE

Birthday Traditions in Jamaica

Miss Lou

'Appy birthday to yuh dear'

Birthday celebrations are always a festivity that warms the heart. Although people don't get a year younger, and with time, responsibilities pile up on their to-do list, they wish to be remembered on this special date.

In Jamaica, birthday celebrations are very similar to many western countries, with birthday cakes, birthday candles, sweets and drinks. However, it's not just that – some traditions in Jamaica are a chapter unto themselves:

Jamaican birthdays come down to flouring! Regardless of age, tradition calls for the birthday boy or girl to be covered with flour, often topping it with some liquid to turn the dusting into cake batter. Friends either organize it during the party or as part of an ambush.

The traditional 'Happy Birthday' song, which has only four short musical phrases and a single repetitive line of words, is sung in many languages all over the world. Jamaicans, however, have a special birthday song whose version was popularized by the Jamaican singer Miss Lou on a television show called "Ring Ding."

Jamaicans are very superstitious. A marriage superstition involves birthdays: if you want a happy, lifelong marriage, don't get married on your birthday as it may bring bad luck!

1 27 Read and listen. Then answer the questions below.

a In what ways are Jamaican birthday celebrations similar to many western countries?

b What birthday prank is played in Jamaica?

c Do Jamaicans sing the traditional Birthday Song? Explain.

d What superstition involves birthdays in Jamaica?

2 INTERFACE How do people celebrate birthdays in your country? Are there any funny birthday pranks? Any superstitions? Share your ideas with your friends.

VOCABULARY 2

Weather and Seasons

1

spring

2

summer

3

fall

4

winter

1 Look at the words in the box. How do you say them in your language?

cloudy cold dry hot rainy snowy
stormy sunny warm wet windy

2 28 Listen and repeat.

3 Which words in activity 1 can you use to describe pictures 1-4?

1: *It's warm, dry and sunny.*
2: ______
3: ______
4: ______

4 Choose the correct words.

a In the Arctic it's **cold / hot**.
b Summer in Mexico is usually **sunny / snowy**.
c People say that the weather in England is **dry / wet**.
d There was no rain last summer so the ground is very **dry / wet**.
e It's **warm / cold** tonight so we can sit outside and eat dinner.
f Last summer in Philadelphia was very **rainy / windy** – we used our umbrellas every day!

PRONUNCIATION

/s/

1 29 Listen and repeat.

scarf snowy socks sometimes
spring stormy summer sunny

2 30 Listen and repeat.

a It's sometimes sunny in spring and it's hot and stormy in summer.
b In winter you need a scarf, gloves and thick socks because sometimes it's snowy.

5 INTERFACE Work in pairs. Ask and answer questions about your favorite season.

What's your favorite season?

It's fall. It's windy and rainy, but I love the color of the trees.

Yes, I agree, but I prefer...

READING 2

1 🔊 31 Read and listen. How old is the Lollapalooza Festival?

____

Come to Lollapalooza... but Bring Your Raincoat!

The Lollapalooza Chicago Festival has been happening every summer, around July / August, since the festival started in 1991! There are going to be over 170 acts this year – rock, pop and dance music and more, including special circus, music and theater acts for children. There are 400,000 tickets but don't wait too long to buy! The tickets are going to go on sale in March, but they usually sell all the tickets in one day. Your parents must send the organizers pictures of you and the other members of your family, because all tickets are personal.

When you go to Chicago for the festival with your family, make sure to look for hotel, Airbnb or other sorts of accommodation in advance.

Also, remember to take clothes for bad weather, like ponchos, boots and especially raincoats, because it usually rains a lot and you must not enter the festival carrying an umbrella! But take your T-shirts and sunscreen too. You never know – it is summer after all!

2 Read the text again. Then write T for *true* or F for *false*.

a ☐ Lollapalooza is only a music festival.

b ☐ There are more than 500,000 tickets.

c ☐ Your parents must send the organizers a picture of you if you want a ticket.

d ☐ It's a good idea to take clothes for good and bad weather.

e ☐ Umbrellas are not allowed at Lollapalooza Chicago Festival.

GRAMMAR 2

must / must not

1 Write (O) if the sentences express *obligation* and (P) if they express *prohibition*.

a ☐ You must not enter the festival carrying an umbrella.

b ☐ Your parents must send the organizers pictures of you and the other members of your family.

2 Look at the chart and check (✓) the correct statements and mark a cross (✗) on the incorrect ones.

affirmative	
I / You	**must** purchase the ticket through Lollapalooza.com.
He / She / It	**must** comply with the search policy.
We / You / They	**must** wear the wristband on the right hand.
negative	
I / You	**must not** carry backpacks.
He / She / It	**must not** bring professional cameras.
We / You / They	**must not** bring pets.

a ☐ *Must* and *must not* are used to express ability.

b ☐ The main verb (after *must* / *must not*) is without 'to.'

c ☐ All pronouns (*I* / *you* / *he* / *she* / *it* / *we* / *you* / *they*) take *must* or *must not* + main verb.

3 Order the words to make sentences.

be / for / must not / late / You / school

You must not be late for school.

a must / Patrons / complete search / prior to entry / agree to / a

____

b do / People / must not / video recording / any / concert / at the

____

c by an adult / Children / be accompanied / must

____

d must not / with / items / enter / You / prohibited

____

GRAMMAR GUIDE page 54

CLIL

ART

Maori Music

In New Zealand, music is an important part of national culture. Wellington is the country's capital, and it is home to the New Zealand Symphony Orchestra, which sometimes tours overseas. The New Zealand School of Music is also based in Wellington.

New Zealand's most famous musical export is the opera singer Kiri Te Kanawa, who has appeared on stage around the world for five decades. She has performed with opera singer Jose Carreras and won many awards, including a Grammy in 1984. A soprano with a high singing voice, Kiri Te Kanawa is of Maori origin.

The Maoris are the native people of New Zealand and their traditional music uses special instruments, such as flutes made of animal bones – like the *nguru* flute – trumpets made of sea shells and drums made with wood and the skin of sharks.

Some of New Zealand's biggest rock, hip-hop and folk groups combine Maori music with European influences.

Nguru – Maori flutes

1 🔊 32 **Read and listen. What are some of the special instruments the Maori people use to make music?**

____

____

2 **Choose the correct answers.**

a Where is the New Zealand School of Music?

1 Auckland
2 Wellington
3 Christchurch

b What type of singer is Jose Carreras?

1 jazz
2 pop
3 opera

c When did Kiri Te Kanawa win a Grammy?

1 1994
2 1984
3 1986

d What type of singer is Kiri Te Kanawa?

1 contralto
2 soprano
3 mezzo-soprano

e Traditional Maori drums are made using...?

1 shark skin
2 animal bones
3 sea shells

VOCABULARY IN PICTURES

Clothes and Accessories

boots

coat

dress

jacket

jeans

scarf

shirt

shorts

skirt

sneakers

T-shirt

sweater

Weather and Seasons

spring

summer

autumn

winter

stormy

sunny

cloudy

cold

dry

hot

rainy

snowy

warm

wet

windy

GRAMMAR GUIDE

be going to

affirmative	contracted form
I am going to wear	'm going to wear
You are going to wear	're going to wear
He / She / It is going to wear	's going to wear
We / You / They are going to wear	're going to wear

- we use *be going to* to talk about plans or intentions in the future
- the form is subject + *be* + *going to* + verb
  I**'m going to** play tennis with my friends.
  You**'re going to** watch a movie.
  She**'s going to** buy some new clothes.

negative	contracted form
I am not going to play	'm not going to play
You are not going to play	aren't going to play
He / She / It is not going to play	isn't going to play
We / You / They are not going to play	aren't going to play

- we use *not* to form the negative
  I**'m not** (am not) **going to** wear sandals.
  He **isn't** (is not) **going to** have a party.
  They **aren't** (are not) **going to** visit their cousins.

questions and short answers	
Am I going to go?	
Yes, I am.	No, I'm not.
Are you going to go?	
Yes, you are.	No, you aren't.
Is he / she / it going to go?	
Yes, he / she / it is.	No, he / she / it isn't.
Are we / you / they going to go?	
Yes, we / you / they are.	No, we / you / they aren't.

- the word order is different in questions
  You **are going to** wear jeans.
  Are you **going to** wear jeans?

must / must not

affirmative
I / You must go
He / She / It must go
We / You / They must go

- we use *must* for obligation
  You **must** wear a uniform at this school.
- we use the same form for all subject pronouns

negative
I / You must not go
He / She / It must not go
We / You / They must not go

- we use *must not* for prohibition
  You **must not** take pictures.
- after *must / must not* we use the verb without *to*
  You **must** bring your ticket.
  You **must not** litter.

PROGRESS CHECK

Clothes

1 Complete the words with vowels.

a s c ___ r f
b s n ___ ___ k ___ r s
c c ___ ___ t
d j ___ c k ___ t
e T - s h ___ r t
f s k ___ r t

Weather and Seasons

2 Look at the map and complete the weather forecast.

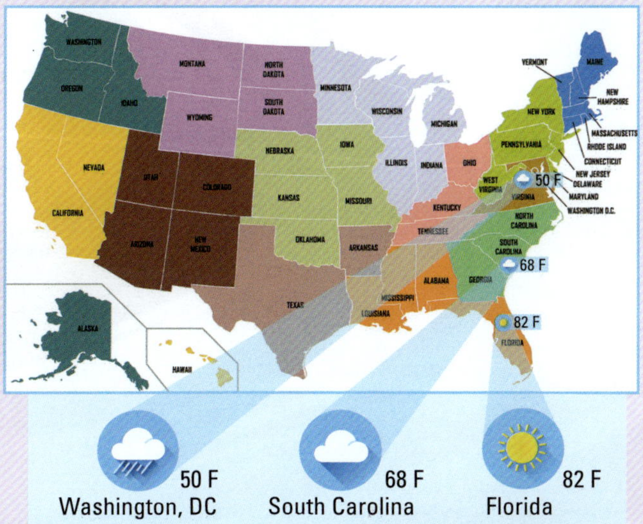

It's June, I know, but in Washington DC today it's going to be **a rainy / windy**. With maximum temperatures of 50 F, it's going to be **b warm / cold**. In South Carolina it's going to be **c warm / hot** but **d stormy / cloudy**. In Florida it's going to be **e cold / hot** and **f sunny / cloudy**.

be going to

3 Order the words to make sentences or questions.

a friends / have / a beach party / My / are / to / going
____

b not / going / wear / I / am / to / that green dress
____

c make / you / a / Are / cake / to / going ?
____

d is / Danny / dance / to / with / going / me
____

must / must not

4 Complete the sentences with *must / must not*.

a You ________ bring glass bottles.
b You ________ only camp in designated areas.
c You ________ have a ticket.
d You ________ light fires.
e You ________ put your trash in the trash cans.

Grammar Buildup 3

1 2 3 4 5 6 7 8

5 Complete the dialogue with the correct form of the verbs in parentheses.

Emily Hi, Olivia! What **a** ____________ you ____________ (do) before I arrived?
Olivia Hi, Emily. I **b** ____________ (put) these old school books in the basement.
Emily Oh yes! It's the last day of school tomorrow.
Olivia I can't wait!
Emily **c** ____________ you ____________ (wear) your black dress tomorrow night?
Olivia No, of course I'm not. Why?
Emily It's the end of year school ball. **d** ____________ you ____________ (go)?
Olivia No, I'm not. I **e** ____________ (go) last year and it **f** ____________ (be) boring.
Emily Olivia, you always **g** ____________ (go). We **h** ____________ (have) a really good time last year. You **i** ____________ (dance) with Jack, remember?
Olivia Yes, I remember. It **j** ____________ (be) awful so I **k** ____________ (not go) tomorrow.
Emily Oh please! Connor, Eric and I **l** ____________ (meet) opposite the school at 7pm. Come with us!

4 Make a Difference

VOCABULARY 1

Jobs

1 Match pictures 1-6 with the jobs in the box. Which jobs aren't in the pictures?

actor	☐	mechanic	☐
architect	☐	nurse	☐
athlete	☐	police officer	☐
electrician	☐	surgeon	☐
engineer	☐	teacher	☐
lifeguard	☐	vet	☐

2 🔊 33 Listen and repeat.

3 Complete the definitions using words from activity 1.

What do we call someone who… designs houses and buildings? *an architect*

a works in a school? ____________

b repairs vehicles and machines? ____________

c designs and builds machines and roads? ____________

d plays professional sports? ____________

e installs and repairs electrical equipment? ____________

f performs in plays and movies? ____________

READING 1

1 34 Read and listen. What do these numbers refer to?

a 1 billion

b 2.5 million

c 24,000

d 5

e 22

f 80

2 What text genre is this?

a ☐ a commercial ad.

b ☐ an institutional ad.

3 Read the text again. Then write T for *true* or F for *false*.

a ☐ Some people travel long distances to find water.

b ☐ World Water Day is celebrated in the UK only.

c ☐ Jamie Cranks is going to queue on March 22.

d ☐ Water.org is going to use Amy's Facebook status.

e ☐ Water.org sends engineers and mechanics from Hollywood to developing countries.

4 Answer the questions.

a What happens on World Water Day?

b What world record do Jamie and his friends hope to break?

c What does Water.org do?

d What is Water.org going to do on World Water Day?

TIP

Learn to recognize prefixes like *un-*. They can help you guess the meaning of a word.

5 Match the words below with their meaning.

a unclear	☐ not needed
b unsafe	☐ dangerous
c unnecessary	☐ not obvious
d unusual	☐ not normal, not ordinary

6 CLASS VOTE Which World Water Day idea do you prefer?

World Water Day
AN INTERNATIONAL DAY OF ACTION

Almost 1 billion people in the world don't have clean water to drink.
2.5 million people don't have access to a toilet.
Every day, 24,000 children under the age of 5 die because of unsafe water.
Many children can't go to school because they need to walk for hours to get water for their family.

March 22 is World Water Day, when there are events around the world focusing on the water crisis. So what should we do on World Water Day?

Stand in a toilet queue*

Jamie Cranks and his friends are from Vancouver. March 22 isn't going to be a normal school day for them because they're going to stand in an unusual queue. Their teacher is going to join them, too! In fact, people in about 80 countries are going to work together to form the world's longest toilet queue.

Donate your Facebook or Twitter status.

Amy, her friends and thousands of other people are going to donate their Facebook and Twitter status to Water.org from March 21 to 26. When Hollywood actor Matt Damon and engineer Gary White created the organization, they had a clear objective: everyone should have access to clean water to drink. Water.org works with local partners to help individuals and communities to meet their own water and sanitation needs. On World Water Day, Water.org is inviting people to donate their Facebook and Twitter statuses to tell millions about the water crisis.

GLOSSARY

*queue: a line of people waiting in a store or similar place

GRAMMAR 1

should (Affirmative and Negative)

1 Read the following sentences. Write GOOD if the recommendation / suggestion given is good and BAD if it is not appropriate.

a [ ] Everyone should have access to clean water to drink.

b [ ] Saving water shouldn't be a real concern.

c [ ] People shouldn't use less water outdoors.

d [ ] People should consider when and how much water is needed.

e [ ] Reusing and recycling water should be considered.

2 Complete the rules below with *should* or *shouldn't*.

a ________ is used to make recommendations and give advice. In a sentence, it gives the meaning of 'It is a good idea.'

b ________ is the negative form and means that you *aren't recommending or advising* something. 'It's NOT a good idea.'

c The sentence structure is: subject + ________ (or ________) + base form of the verb.

3 Complete the chart with *should* or *shouldn't*.

affirmative		
I / You	________	save water.
He / She / It	________	consider saving water.
We / You / They	________	recycle water.
negative		
I / You	________	waste water.
He / She / It	________	be left out.
We / You / They	________	drink unsafe water.

4 Look at the information about saving water at home. Complete the sentences with *should* or *shouldn't*.

a You ________ turn off the faucet when you brush your teeth.

b You ________ take long showers.

c You ________ fix a dripping faucet.

d You ________ water your garden with a hose.

e You ________ run washing machines when they are not full.

5 Read the situations below and give people some advice / recommendation.

a You are walking down a street and you see two kids throwing trash on the sidewalk.

____

____

____

____

b Your neighbor is watering his plants with a hose. He's been doing it for two hours!

____

____

____

____

c Your friend is doing the dishes under constantly flowing water.

____

____

____

____

d Your little brother is flushing the toilet nonstop!

____

____

____

____

6 Look at the pictures below. Say what people should or shouldn't do. Use the cues to complete the sentences.

a The kids (✗) ______________________.

b People (✓) ______________________ in parks.

c Everybody (✓) ______________________ when leaving the house.

d People (✗) ______________________.

GRAMMAR GUIDE page 68

LISTENING

Heroes

1 You are going to listen to Ed, Rosie and Vicky talking about their heroes. First, look at the pictures. What do you think these people do?

____

____

2 🔊 35 Listen and match the person with their hero.

a Ed ☐ Aunt Chantal
b Rosie ☐ Mr. Benson
c Vicky ☐ Tom Daley

3 🔊 35 Listen again and choose the correct words.

a Tom Daley won the world championship in **2008 / 2009**.

b Tom also helps **his local school / a charity**.

c Aunt Chantal's going to work in a camp for **700 / 100,000** people.

d She's going to work with **children / families**.

e Mr. Benson **is / isn't** going to retire next year.

4 🔊 35 Listen again and answer the questions.

a How old was Tom when he competed in the Beijing Olympics?

____

b Where is Aunt Chantal going to work?

____

c What other job does Mr. Benson have?

____

5 Who is your hero? Why?

____

____

CULTURAL FACT

The BBC gives awards to athletes every year. Tom Daley is the first person to win the Young Sports Personality of the Year award more than once.

SPEAKING

World Water Day

36 Robert and Peter are talking about World Water Day. Listen and complete the dialogue.

You know, Peter, today, in class we talked about how essential water is not only to put an end to thirst and protect **a** ________, but also for supporting economic, social and **b** ______________.

What exactly did you discuss?

Well, first we talked about **c** ______________, which puts people at risk of contracting lots of **d** ________ and dying...

Sure thing! And there's also the fact that unsafe water, **e** ______________ and hygiene cause thousands of deaths every year.

f ______________, an event celebrated every March 22, focuses on raising awareness and inspiring action to tackle water and sanitation issues.

Oh, I've heard about it! I think it's an awareness day which brings to light the inequality of access to **g** ______________, particularly in developing countries.

Yeah, I **h** ________ that an abundance of quality water can change people's jobs and **i** ________ for the better!

We **j** ________ do something to be part of it! How about starting at home and school?

Good idea! We could organize a **k** ______________!

Well, then, let's tell our friends and teachers about it.

FUNCTIONAL LANGUAGE

Giving Opinions and Suggestions
I think...
I imagine...
We should...

Speaking Task

Write a dialogue between you and a friend.

Step 1

Choose one of the following events to write about or use an idea of your own.

Step 2

Think about what to say. Search for information about the event.

I learned that...
In class we talked about / discussed...
It is an event celebrated...
It aims to...

Think about what your friend is going to say.

I also learned that...
I imagine...
I think...
We should / shouldn't ...

Step 3

Work with a partner. Write your dialogue. Follow the conversation above as a guide.

Step 4

Take turns practicing your dialogue.

CULTURE

Trinidad and Tobago and Its Cultural Relationship with the Ocean

Trinidad and Tobago, a two-island nation in the southern Caribbean, is home to nearly 1.4 million people whose existence is tied to the sea. Trinidadians ('Trinis,' as citizens proudly call themselves) and Tobagonians say they are blessed with a particular phenomenon in that their country consists of 15 times more ocean than land area. They firmly believe they have to pay attention to the marine and coastal environments, home to fish, sharks, turtles, coral reefs and numerous marine organisms.

Trinidadians understand that oceans are part of what it means to be a Trini. There is a traditional ritual when a baby is born: at a specific time, babies are taken to the beach to dip their feet in the saltwater so that they can grow up healthy. When you are sick or there is something wrong with you, such as an upset stomach, you should go to the beach to drink some of the salt water.

Oceans play an essential role in human well-being, producing half of the oxygen for life on the planet. Therefore, Trinidadians and Tobagonians are aware of the importance of sustainable development, which includes action on ocean-related issues such as reducing plastic pollution and addressing the impact of climate change. Protecting the ocean to protect humanity is their goal.

1 37 **Read and listen to the information. Then check (✓) the correct information.**

a Trinidad and Tobago...

- [ ] has an intimate relationship with the sea.
- [ ] consists of one island in the southern Caribbean.

b Trinis feel...

- [ ] the marine and coastal environments aren't of vital importance.
- [ ] they are blessed by living in a region where the ocean covers more area than the land.

c When babies are born...

- [ ] they are taken to the sea to dip their feet in the saltwater.
- [ ] they are blessed by a local priest.

d Trinis believe...

- [ ] boiling and bathing in seawater can heal many diseases.
- [ ] drinking sea water helps heal an upset stomach.

e Trinidadians and Tobagonians...

- [ ] know the importance of sustainable development.
- [ ] think they don't need to worry about actions on ocean-related issues.

2 **In your country, are there any cultural traditions related to nature? Describe (it / one of them) and its impact on people's lives.**

____

____

VOCABULARY 2

Health Problems

1 Read the words in the box. Which words can you use to describe pictures a-d?

broken arm	☐	insect bite	☐
cold	☐	sick	☐
cough	☐	sore throat	☐
cut	☐	stomachache	☐
earache	☐	temperature	☐
headache	☐		

2 38 Listen and repeat.

a

b

c

d

3 Choose the correct words.

a A **headache / stomachache** is when you have a pain in your head.

b He went outside without a coat in January and now he has **a cold / an insect bite**.

c She has a **sore throat / stomachache** because she ate her dinner very quickly.

d I was talking all day yesterday and now I have **a sore throat / a broken arm**.

4 Answer the questions. Use the words in the box.

drink water have a cough drop lie down put on a bandage take an aspirin

What do you do when you have…

… a headache? *I take an aspirin and I lie down.*

a … a sore throat? ______________________

b … a cough? ______________________

c … a cut? ______________________

d … a temperature? ______________________

5 INTERFACE Work in pairs. Ask and answer the questions in activity 4.

READING 2

1 39 Read and listen to the interview. What does John Martin do in his free time?

____

2 What is John Martin's advice for these situations?

a Someone feels tired.

____

b Someone has a broken leg.

____

c You need to speak to the police.

____

d Someone has an insect bite.

____

e Someone has a temperature.

____

Mountain Rescue!

John Martin works for the rescue service in the National Park.

Q: John, is this your only job?

A: No, I'm an electrician, but in my free time I'm a volunteer for the rescue service.

Q: What are the most common problems?

A: A very common problem is exhaustion. If someone in your group looks tired, you should all rest. You should also carry high energy food, like chocolate.

Q: And what should I do if someone has a broken leg or arm? Should I move them?

A: No, you shouldn't move them. You should call for help.

Q: Who should I contact?

A: You should call 911 to speak to the police. While you wait, you should keep the person warm.

Q: What about for minor things like insect bites?

A: Use cold water or a special cream, but if the person has a temperature you should contact a doctor.

GRAMMAR 2

should (Questions and Short Answers)

1 **Read the questions below and choose the best answer for each one of them.**

a Should you cover your mouth when you cough?

☐ Yes, we should.
☐ No, we shouldn't.

b Mark has broken his leg. Should he move it?

☐ Yes, he should.
☐ No, he shouldn't.

c The kids are sick. Should they go swimming?

☐ Yes, they should.
☐ No, they shouldn't.

d Jane has a sore throat and a cough. Should she go to the doctor?

☐ Yes, she should.
☐ No, she shouldn't.

2 **Complete the rules below with the words from the box.**

affirmative questions short answers

a In __________, *should* comes before the subject.

b In __________, use *should* (__________) and *shouldn't* (negative).

3 **Refer to activities 1 and 2 and complete the chart below.**

questions and short answers
__________ I / you go to the doctor? Yes, I / you __________. No, I / you __________.
__________ he / she / it move the person? Yes, he / she / it __________. No, he / she / it __________.
__________ we / you / they go swimming? Yes, we / you / they __________. No, we / you / they __________.

4 **Write complete questions.**

I have a terrible cold. stay at home / go to school?
Should I stay at home or should I go to school?

a I always feel terrible on buses. sit at the front / sit at the back?

____

b It's my mom's birthday. buy her a present / make her dinner?

____

c My friends want to learn a new language. study Chinese / study German?

____

d We want to try a new activity. go paintballing / go karting?

____

5 **Answer the questions in activity 4 using *should* and *shouldn't*.**

____
____
____
____

6 **Read the information below. Then answer the questions that follow.**

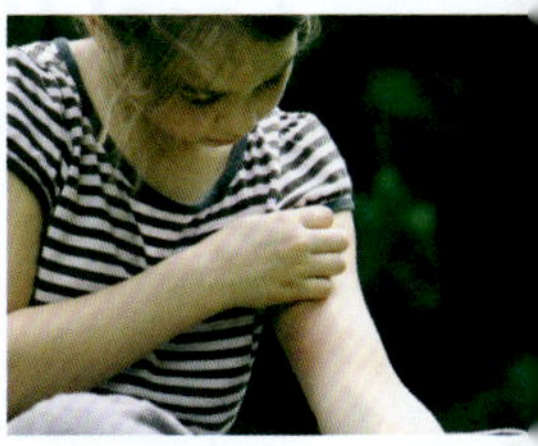

There are several things you can do to relieve pain in case of insect bites or stings. Here are a few:

- Don't panic!
- Apply an ice pack to a bite or sting for 15 to 20 minutes once an hour for the first 6 hours.
- Elevate the area of the bite or sting to decrease swelling.
- Do not use any cream on children younger than age 2 without a doctor's prescription.

In case of an insect bite or sting...

a Should we panic?

____

b Should people apply an ice pack to the sting for 15 to 20 minutes once an hour for the first 6 hours?

____

c Should we elevate the area of the bite or sting to decrease swelling?

____

d Should adults use a cream on children younger than age 2 without a doctor's prescription?

____

GRAMMAR GUIDE page 68

WRITING

A Letter

1 🔊 40 Read and listen. Who are Haley and Matt's heroes?

Local Heroes

Tell us about your hero. This could be a member of your family, a friend or someone who works in your town.

Hi!
A few years ago, my grandmother was in North Bridge Hospital for several weeks. The doctors told her, 'You should change your habits!' She began to eat a more healthy diet and she also started to play sports. Next week she's going to run a half marathon to raise money for the hospital. She's also going to work at the hospital as a volunteer. She's going to talk to patients who don't usually have visitors. What a hero!
Haley, Sacramento.

Hello!
I'm going to nominate our vet, Mr. Rodgers. Last week, our dog Maggie jumped off our balcony. She had a broken leg and a terrible cut on her face, too. Mr. Rodgers was very patient and he was also very kind. Maggie's going to be fine. Thank you, Mr. Rodgers!
Matt, Wichita.

LANGUAGE FOCUS

also* and *too
Use *also* and *too* to add new information and make your writing more interesting.

She *also* started to play sports.
He was patient and he was *also* very kind.
Maggie had a terrible cut on her face, *too*.

2 Look at the Language Focus. Where do *too* and *also* go in the sentence?

___

___

3 Rewrite the sentences including the words in parentheses.

She had a headache. She had a temperature. (too)
She had a headache. She had a temperature, too.

a We should run a marathon. We should climb Ben Nevis. (also)

___

___

b He cleaned the kitchen and the living room. He washed the floors. (also)

___

___

c They're going to look after children. They're going to look after animals. (too)

___

___

d My uncle is friendly. He is kind. (also)

___

___

4 Write a letter about your hero. Follow these steps.

Writing a Letter

Step 1 > PLAN
Make notes under three headings:
a Who is your hero?
b Why is he / she your hero?
c What is he / she going to do next?

Step 2 > WRITE
Write a first draft. Use your notes from Step 1 and the letters on this page to help you.

Step 3 > CHECK
Check your work. Try to include *too* and *also*.

Step 4 > WRITE
Write your final copy and hand in your work.

VOCABULARY IN PICTURES

Jobs

Health Problems

broken arm

cold

cough

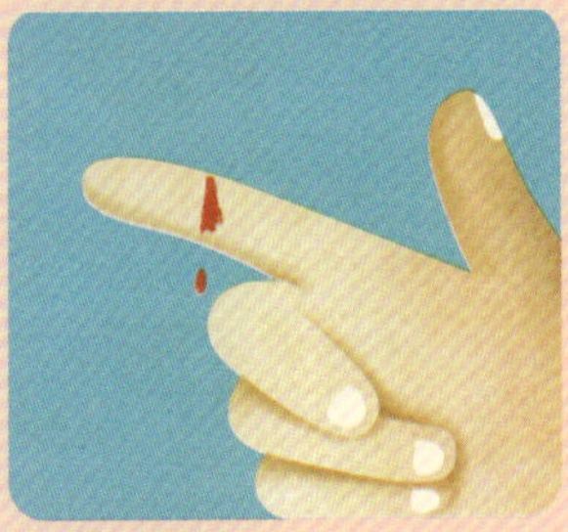
cut

earache

headache

insect bite

sick

sore throat

stomachache

temperature

GRAMMAR GUIDE

should

affirmative and negative		
+	I / You / He / She / It We / You / They	should go.
–	I / You / He / She / It We / You / They	shouldn't go.

questions and short answers	
Should I / you / go?	
Yes, I should.	No, I shouldn't.
Should he / she / it go?	
Yes, he should.	No, he shouldn't.
Should we / you / they go?	
Yes, we should.	No, we shouldn't.

- we use *should* and *shouldn't* to ask for and give advice and recommendations
  You **should** see the doctor.
  You **shouldn't** go to the party.
- the form is the same for all subject pronouns
  He **should** stop and rest.
  We **shouldn't** move.

PROGRESS CHECK

Jobs

1 Identify the jobs.

a

m__________

b

p__________ o__________

c

a__________

d
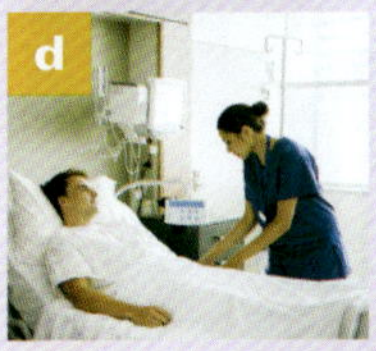
n__________

e
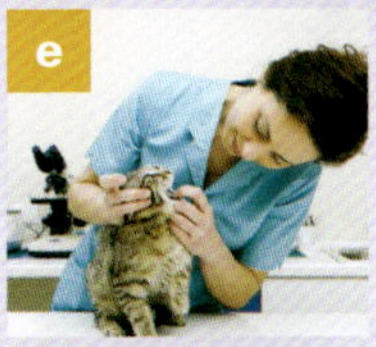
v__________

f

e__________

Health Problems

2 Match the symptoms with the cures.

a I have a sore throat.
b I have a temperature.
c He has a broken leg.
d I have a mosquito bite.
e I have a horrible cut.

☐ Here's some cream.
☐ Have a cough drop!
☐ Would you like a bandage?
☐ You should take an aspirin.
☐ You shouldn't move him.

should

3 Complete the sentences with *should* or *shouldn't*.

a I want to be an architect, but I'm not very good at drawing.
You __________ (✗) worry about drawing.
You __________ (✓) learn to use a drawing program on a computer.

b My sister wants to play soccer, but her friends say hockey is better.
She __________ (✓) listen to her friends.
She __________ (✗) play soccer.

c My friends are going to climb a mountain.
They __________ (✗) continue if they are tired. They __________ (✓) wear comfortable shoes.

d I have a headache and a temperature, but I want to meet my friends.
You __________ (✓) lie down. You __________ (✗) meet your friends.

Grammar Buildup 4

1 2 3 4 5 6 7 8

4 Complete the dialogue with the correct form of the verbs in parentheses.

Mom: You **a** __________ (look) awful. What **b** __________ (be) wrong?
Lou: I **c** __________ (run) home when I **d** __________ (fall).
Mom: Oh dear. **e** __________ it __________ (hurt)?
Lou: Yes, and I **f** __________ (play) soccer tomorrow. What should I **g** __________ (do)?
Mom: You should **h** __________ (put) some ice on it. Can you **i** __________ (move) it?
Lou: No, not really. It **j** __________ (feel) really painful.
Mom: Let's **k** __________ (call) the doctor.
Lou: OK. **l** __________ you __________ (have) the number?
Mom: Yes, here you go.
Lou: Thanks, Mom.

Review 2

VOCABULARY

GRAMMAR

Across

3 I have a terrible ...! I have a headache, sore throat and temperature. I need to stay home today!

4 He ate too much. That's why he had a ... and couldn't go to school.

5 On ... days, use an umbrella.

7 Claire is going to take her dog Tom to the ... because he is sick.

9 A plastic ... should be prepared to operate on a patient's body.

10 A good ... should be prepared to save swimmers who are in danger.

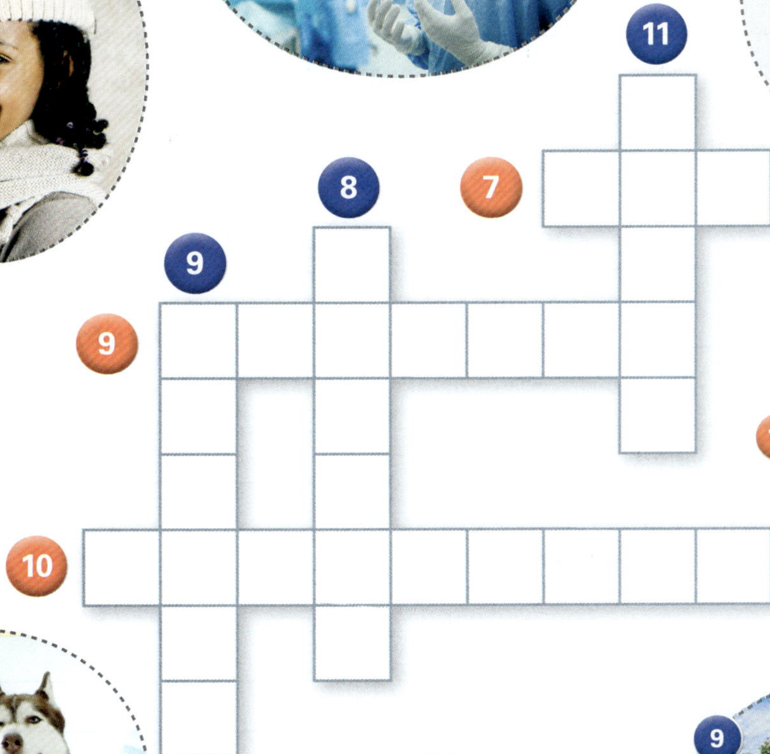

Down

1 A pain in your head is a ...

2 A ... is a warm piece of clothing that covers your upper body and arms.

3 I can hardly see the sun because the sky is ...

6 It's cold! You should wear this ... around your neck to avoid getting a sore throat.

8 He had a ... arm after he fell off his bike.

9 Let's enjoy the beautiful flowers of ..., my favorite season!

11 I usually wear a pair of ... and a white T-shirt.

Review 2

VOCABULARY | GRAMMAR

be going to

1 **Write affirmative sentences with *be going to.***

my dad / arrive home late
My dad is going to arrive home late.

a we / live in Scotland
____

b my football team / win the game
____

c it / be cloudy
____

d they / wear sneakers
____

e I / study for my exams
____

f my classmates / have a party
____

2 **Rewrite the sentences in the negative form.**

I'm going to visit my grandmother.
I'm not going to visit my grandmother.

a They're going to read a book.
____

b Harry's going to dance at the school ball.
____

c We're going to have a terrible time.
____

d Eva's going to walk to school.
____

e You're going to call your cousin.
____

3 **Complete the questions with *be going to* and the verbs in the box.**

drink fly hit meet
~~play~~ sunbathe watch

Are you *going to play* basketball later?

a _______ your mom _______ orange juice for breakfast?

b _______ your friends _______ TV tonight?

c _______ your uncle _______ the airplane?

d _______ we _______ on the beach?

e _______ you _______ the ball?

f _______ I _______ you in front of the park?

4 **Write short answers for the questions in activity 3.**

✓ *Yes, I am.*

a ✗ _______________

b ✗ _______________

c ✓ _______________

d ✓ _______________

e ✓ _______________

f ✗ _______________

must / must not

5 **Complete the sentences with *must* or *must not.***

You *must not* play basketball inside the classroom.

a We _______ speak English in our French class.

b I _______ do my homework every day.

c They _______ talk loudly in the library.

d Olympic athletes _______ train every day.

e You _______ take a shower before you enter the swimming pool.

f We _______ write on our desks.

should

6 **Complete the sentences with *should* or *shouldn't*.**

I feel tired and I have a headache. I think I *should* lie down.

a Henry has a terrible stomachache. He ________ eat any more cake.

b It's my friend's birthday. I ________ call her.

c That old woman wants to cross the road. We ________ help her.

d The party starts at 7:30pm. You ________ be late.

e They use the laptop every day. They ________ sell it.

f I can't understand you. You ________ speak more slowly.

7 **Order the words to make questions.**

I / a cream / use / Should ?

Should I use a cream?

a study / my brother / Russian / Should ?

____

b buy / Should / new speakers / I ?

____

c we / fly / Should / to Galicia ?

____

d money / they / Should / borrow ?

____

e a surgeon / Rachel / be / Should ?

____

f this water / Should / we / drink ?

____

8 **Answer the questions in activity 7 according to the clues given.**

I'm allergic.

No, I shouldn't.

a He is passionate about languages.

____

b My allowance money is all gone.

____

c Tickets are at a super sale discount.

____

d The interest rates are very low now.

____

e She is scared of blood.

____

f It looks a bit yellow.

____

9 **Complete the how-to list using *should* or *shouldn't*.**

BuzzFeed

News Testes Menu

What you *should* or *shouldn't* do when you hurt yourself while training

1. First of all, you **a** ________ panic! That can only make things worse. You **b** ________ take a deep breath and face the situation.
2. If you're on the street or at any unsafe place, you **c** ________ first check if you can walk to move to a safe place.
3. You **d** ________ ask for help to leave the unsafe spot in case you have any difficulties walking.
4. Don't try to move the injured body part on your own. You **e** ________ call your local emergency services.
5. After seeing the doctor, you **f** ________ follow their instructions carefully to heal soon!

Teens in the Tech World

- **What part does technology play in your life?**
- **Does it bring you more positive or negative things? How?**

1 Look at the picture on the right. Do you see yourself as being influenced positively or negatively by media and technology? Discuss with a classmate.

2 Media has a huge influence on teens' lives. Read and reflect on the sentences below and mark + for positive and – for negative.

a ☐ Teens can develop awareness about the world when exposed to various media outlets.

b ☐ Media can help teens make new friends from all parts of the world and be more communicative.

c ☐ Media may show a distorted body image, causing teens to want to achieve the 'perfect' body shape.

d ☐ Celebrities inspire teens and may motivate them to do good things, such as reading, eating right, etc.

e ☐ Spending too much time in front of a TV, cell phone or computer may lead to obesity.

f ☐ Video games help teens develop their coordination and motor skills.

3 Do you know the minimum age necessary to take part in any of the social media communities below? Why do you think there is a minimum age requirement?

___

___

4 **Have you ever used the internet to help a cause? Check off (✓) if you have. Then give some more detail.**

a ☐ Volunteered on a campaign. Which one?

____

____

b ☐ Helped a non-profit organization. How?

____

____

c ☐ Promoted an event to raise money for charity. What kind of event?

____

____

A Debate on Cyber Habits

You and a group of friends have decided to raise awareness about internet safety and solidarity in your school community. The idea is to generate a rich debate with students of all ages and school staff and, if possible, reach an agreement as to what practices could be avoided or encouraged in the school environment.

Doing

1 Decide which issues are most sensitive in your community. For example, cyber bullying, children safety on the web, privacy, cyber consumerism etc.

2 Divide the class into groups so that each group is responsible for researching information on one of the issues raised in step 1.

3 Organize the most relevant information about the issue discussed and write a few proposals, using the school community as the target audience. For example:

1. Create a school channel to report cyber bullying.

4 Share your ideas with the other groups and divide tasks in order to organize the debate with students from other grades and with school staff.

Presenting

5 One or more groups should be responsible for announcing the debate across all school communities, both online and also in posters to be hung on the school bulletin boards.

6 One or more groups should organize the debate, which involves deciding who are going to be the moderators, providing and setting up audio equipment, booking the room / auditorium / outdoor area and informing school staff and security.

7 If contradictory actions are proposed during the debate, the mediators should organize a voting system – for example, students and staff in favor of the proposal should raise their hands.

8 One or more groups should be responsible for writing down the **minutes** of the debate, that is, a document with the most important topics discussed and the decisions reached in common. Then the group(s) should make it public within the school community.

Reflecting

9 Did the school reach a conclusion that the internet can be used for good deeds? Why (not)?

10 What issues raised in the debate do you agree with the most?

11 What else can you use the experience from the debate for?

Irregular Verbs

78

Infinitive	Simple Past	Past Participle
be /bi/	was / were /wɑz/, /wɜr/	been /bin/, /bɪn/
begin /bɪ'gɪn/	began /bɪ'gæn/	begun /bɪ'gʌn/
break /breɪk/	broke /broʊk/	broken /'broʊkən/
bring /brɪŋ/	brought /brɔt/	brought /brɔt/
build /bɪld/	built /bɪlt/	built /bɪlt/
buy /baɪ/	bought /bɔt/	bought /bɔt/
choose /tʃuz/	chose /tʃoʊz/	chosen /'tʃoʊz(ə)n/
come /kʌm/	came /keɪm/	come /kʌm/
do /du/	did /dɪd/	done /dʌn/
drink /drɪŋk/	drank /dræŋk/	drunk /drʌŋk/
drive /draɪv/	drove /droʊv/	driven /'drɪv(ə)n/
eat /it/	ate /eɪt/	eaten /'it(ə)n/
fall /fɔl/	fell /fel/	fallen /'fɔlən/
find /faɪnd/	found /faʊnd/	found /faʊnd/
fly /flaɪ/	flew /flu/	flown /floʊn/
forget /fər'get/	forgot /fər'gɑt/	forgotten /fər'gɑt(ə)n/
get /get/	got /gɑt/	got /gɑt/, gotten /'gɑt(ə)n/
give /gɪv/	gave /geɪv/	given /'gɪv(ə)n/
go /goʊ/	went /went/	gone /gɔn/
have /hæv/	had /həd/	had /həd/
hear /hɪr/	heard /hɜrd/	heard /hɜrd/
know /noʊ/	knew /nu/	known /noʊn/
learn /lɜrn/	learnt / learned /lɜrnt/, /'lɜrnəd/	learnt / learned /lɜrnt/, /'lɜrnəd/
leave /liv/	left /left/	left /left/
lose /luz/	lost /lɔst/	lost /lɔst/
make /meɪk/	made /meɪd/	made /meɪd/
meet /mit/	met /met/	met /met/
pay /peɪ/	paid /peɪd/	paid /peɪd/
put /pʊt/	put /pʊt/	put /pʊt/
read /rid/	read /red/	read /red/
run /rʌn/	ran /ræn/	run /rʌn/
say /seɪ/	said /sed/	said /sed/
see /si/	saw /sɔ/	seen /sin/
sell /sel/	sold /soʊld/	sold /soʊld/
sing /sɪŋ/	sang /sæŋ/	sung /sʌŋ/
sit /sɪt/	sat /sæt/	sat /sæt/
speak /spik/	spoke /spoʊk/	spoken /'spoʊkən/
take /teɪk/	took /tʊk/	taken /'teɪkən/
teach /titʃ/	taught /tɔt/	taught /tɔt/
tell /tel/	told /toʊld/	told /toʊld/
think /θɪŋk/	thought /θɔt/	thought /θɔt/
wear /wer/	wore /wɔr/	worn /wɔrn/
win /wɪn/	won /wʌn/	won /wʌn/
write /raɪt/	wrote /roʊt/	written /'rɪt(ə)n/

Workbook

CONTENTS

Starter

Free-time Activities

1 Complete the sentences with the words in the box.

do (2x)	go to (2x)	play (2x)

a My parents ________ volunteer work at an urban wildlife rehabilitation center.

b I love to ________ video games with my younger cousins at my grandma's house.

c John and Mike ________ judo and it really helps them to be more focused and relaxed.

d One of my favorite free-time activities is to ________ my guitar.

e My friends and I like to ________ the movies on Saturday evenings.

f We often meet our neighbors when we ________ the gym.

Character Adjectives and Formation of Adverbs

2 Complete with the opposite adjectives and write their adverb form.

a	dishonest	*honest*	*honestly*
b	bad	________	________
c	sad	________	________
d	shy	________	________
e	talkative	________	________

3 Complete the adverbs with the missing letters.

a ___ u i ___ ___ l ___

b h a ___ ___ ___ l y

c c ___ r ___ f ___ ___ l y

d ___ n g ___ ___ ___ y

Rooms, Furniture and Gadgets

4 Label the furniture and gadgets and the room where you usually find them.

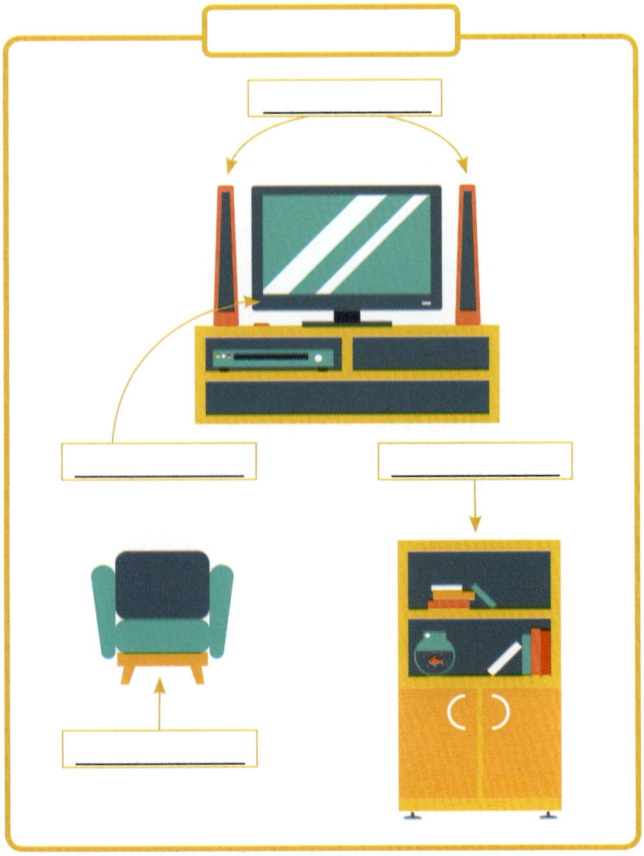

Places to Visit

5 Write the place each person should visit, according to their interests.

art gallery   campground   cave   safari park

a Maria wants to observe freely roaming animals: ____________________

b Edward is fascinated by paintings and sculptures: ____________________

c Lavaughn is really curious about underground formations: ____________________

d Jeremy likes nature and wants to learn some outdoor skills: ____________________

Comparatives and Superlatives

6 Look at the picture and complete the sentences with the comparative or the superlative form of the words in the box.

long   old   short   tall   young

a Dean is __________ person in the family.

b Sarah's hair is __________ than Karen's.

c Frank is __________ than Lisa.

d Laura is Dean's and Sarah's __________ daughter.

e Sue is __________ than Larry.

Simple Present and Present Progressive

7 Complete the questions with the simple present or present progressive. Then find the answers in the box.

I thought of something really funny.
On the weekends.   Yes, I do.
To the library.   No, I'm studying.

a Where ________ you ________ (go)?
____

b When ________ you usually ________ (play) video games?
____

c ________ you ________ (watch) TV now?
____

d ________ you usually ________ (go) to school in the morning?
____

e Why ________ you ________ (laugh)?
____

Simple Past and Past Progressive

8 Write questions for the answers.

a ____________________
____

Last night I had dinner at 9:00.

b ____________________
____

When the teacher arrived I was talking to my friend.

c ____________________
____

Yesterday I watched the new episode of *Greenhouse Academy* on TV.

d ____________________
____

The person I was talking to is my cousin Dan.

e ____________________
____

The most interesting book I read last year was *Around the World in Eighty Days*, by Jules Verne.

1 Technology

VOCABULARY 1

IT Activities

1 Order the letters and write the words.

d s n e a n i m l a e *send an email*

a d a e r a n o k b o e- ____________

b i t n p r a m t u n e o d c ____________

c l o d u p a a e d i o v l c p i ____________

d l u p g i n a h a f s l r v i e d ____________

2 Look at the pictures and find six IT activities in the wordsnake.

a

b

c

d

e

f

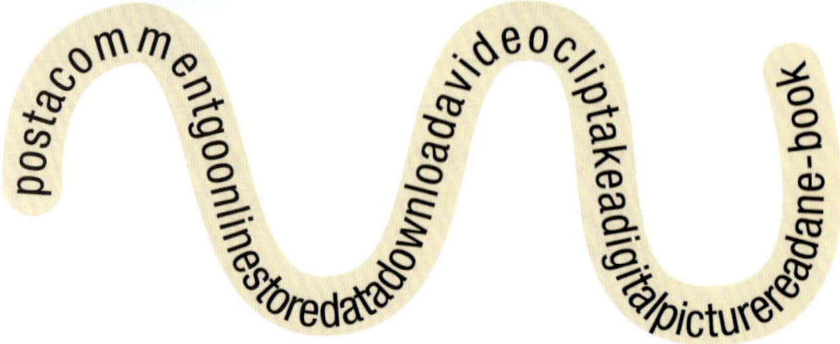

3 Match the verbs with the phrases.

a	[*3*] scan	**1**	a blog
b	[ ] write	**2**	a phone call
c	[ ] charge	**3**	a picture
d	[ ] play	**4**	a video game
e	[ ] make	**5**	a cell phone

4 Complete the sentences with the words in the box.

blog charge data online post print read scan send store ~~upload~~

I have a video clip on my camera. How can I *upload* it onto the internet?

a There's an interesting story on this website. I want to ____________ a comment.

b I always ____________ my cell phone at night when I go to bed.

c I love movies. I have a ____________ called Movie Zone and I write two posts on it every week.

d I don't want to lose this ____________. I have it on my computer and on my flash drive.

e Can you ____________ music files on your cell phone?

f When you buy a ticket ____________, you usually need to ____________ a copy.

g These are my grandma's old black and white pictures. I want to ____________ them and give them back to her.

h I need the PDF files from that book to write my part in the project. Can you ____________ them to me via email, please?

i This e-book is too long for me to ____________ it on my cell phone. I need to get an e-reader.

GRAMMAR 1

Review: Simple Past

1 Underline the correct words.

The video clip <u>**was**</u> / **were** really boring.

- **a** Where **was** / **were** you last night?
- **b** Who **was** / **were** that girl at the internet café?
- **c** Adam and Layla **wasn't** / **weren't** pleased about the comments on their blog.
- **d** There **was** / **were** an amazing picture on that website.
- **e** My digital camera **wasn't** / **weren't** a birthday present.
- **f** **Was** / **Were** there a lot of free games on that site?

2 Complete the sentences with *was* or *were*.

How old ___*were*___ you in 2013?

- **a** Where ________ Andy's flash drive?
- **b** Where ________ you during the video conference?
- **c** I ________ annoyed with her about the pictures of me on Facebook.
- **d** There ________ a great blog about zombie movies by a French guy.
- **e** What ________ Kate's digital pictures like?

3 Correct the sentences. Write one negative and one affirmative sentence.

My video clips were on my digital camera. (✗ cell phone)

My video clips weren't on my digital camera.

They were on my cell phone.

- **a** My cell phone was under the bed. (✗ the sofa)

  ____

  ____

- **b** We were at the computer store yesterday afternoon. (✗ park)

  ____

  ____

- **c** The text message was from Adam. (✗ Alice)

  ____

  ____

- **d** The games on that site were terrible. (✗ great)

  ____

  ____

4 Complete the text with the simple past form of the verbs in parentheses.

We ___*visited*___ (visit) the Computer History Museum in California last year. First, we **a** ________ (watch) a movie about the history of computers. They **b** ________ (show) us a strange computer from 1939 – the Atanasoff-Berry computer. It **c** ________ (look) like lots of light bulbs on a metal plate! In the movie there was also a huge calculator from 1940. They **d** ________ (call) it the Complex Number Calculator. George Stibitz **e** ________ (design) it. It **f** ________ (use) telephone wires to send the calculations to a machine in another city. After the movie, we **g** ________ (walk) around the museum with a guide. She **h** ________ (talk) about all the old computers.

5 Complete the text with the simple past form of the regular verbs in the box.

~~arrive~~ call charge chat learn play stay store try use

My new cell phone ___*arrived*___ by mail yesterday. I **a** ________ at home in the afternoon and **b** ________ how to use it. First, I **c** ________ the battery. Then I **d** ________ all the data from my old phone on it – names, telephone numbers and email addresses. Then I **e** ________ Marianne and **f** ________ with her for ten minutes. After that, I **g** ________ two games. They were both excellent! Then I **h** ________ taking some pictures with the camera. It's fantastic. Finally, I **i** ________ a special flash memory card to upload some pictures and music files from my computer. Technology! I love it!

6 Complete the text with the simple past form of the irregular verbs in parentheses.

I ___*had*___ (have) an amazing vacation last year. My grandmother **a** ________ (give) me some money and I **b** ________ (go) traveling with my friend, Adam. Our vacation **c** ________ (begin) badly because Adam **d** ________ (lose) his passport in Paris. Luckily, the police **e** ________ (find) it for him. We **f** ________ (take) a train from Paris to the south of France. Then we **g** ________ (get) a boat to the island of Corsica. We **h** ________ (swim) every day, **i** ________ (eat) lots of delicious French food and **j** ________ (make) friends with some Spanish people at the campground. Then we **k** ________ (fly) back to Austin.

7 Match the sentence beginnings with the endings. Write the sentences in the simple past negative form.

a [3] I (not visit) you
b [ ] I (not call) you
c [ ] We (not watch) all of the movie
d [ ] I (not scan) his pictures
e [ ] We (not chat) to her online
f [ ] We (not go) to the internet café

1 because I (not have) my cell phone.
2 because we (not like) it.
3 because I (not have) your address.
4 because we (not know) her.
5 because he (not want) me to.
6 because we (not need) to.

a *I didn't visit you because I didn't have your address.*
b ________________________________
c ________________________________
d ________________________________
e ________________________________
f ________________________________

8 Complete the questions and answers with the simple past form of the verbs in parentheses.

Ross Where ___*did you get*___ (you / get) your new cell phone?
Jane I **a** ____________ (buy) it at the store on Creekside Way.
Ross How much **b** ____________ (it / cost)?
Jane I **c** ____________ (pay) US$200 for it.
Pete **d** ____________ (you / call) Ellie?
Carol No, I **e** ____________ (send) her a text.
Pete What **f** ____________ (you / say) in it?
Carol I **g** ____________ (invite) her to a concert.
Sue When **h** ____________ (Jo / break) her e-reader?
Paul She **i** ____________ (not break) it. She **j** ____________ (leave) it at her cousin's house on Saturday.
Guy When **k** ____________ (Tom download) all this music?
Jen He **l** ____________ (do) it yesterday. It **m** ____________ (not take) long.

9 Write a short answer and an extra sentence for each question.

Did you wake up early yesterday?
Yes, I did. (short answer)
I woke up at 6:30. (extra sentence)
No, I didn't. (short answer)
I woke up at 10:30. (extra sentence)

a Did you have breakfast this morning?
____

b Did your teacher give you homework yesterday?
____

c Did you get any text messages yesterday?
____

d Did you leave your flash drive in the school computer?
____

VOCABULARY 2

Jobs

1 Match the jobs with the pictures.

a [5] construction worker
b [ ] scientist
c [ ] mailman
d [ ] doctor
e [ ] fireman
f [ ] policewoman
g [ ] lawyer
h [ ] artist

1

2

3

4

5

6

7

8
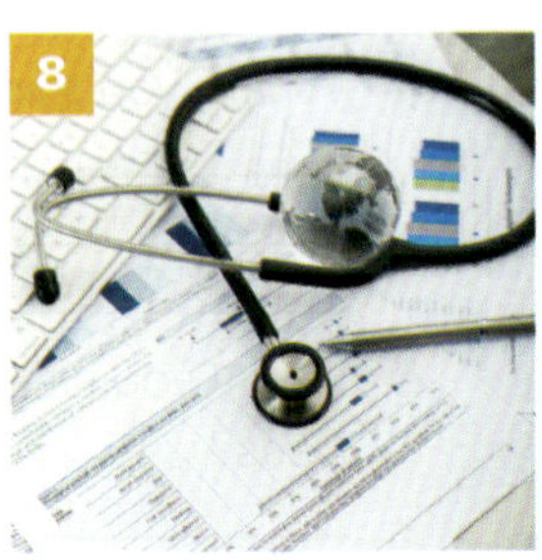

2 Match the word beginnings and endings to make jobs.

a journal [ ] ian
b politic [ ] er
c research [ ] ist
d techni [ ] cian

3 Read what the people say and write their jobs.

Open your mouth please. I need to check your throat.
doctor

a Someone dropped a cigarette and that's how the fire started. We managed to put it out and luckily nobody died.
______

b The police say he did it. He says he didn't do it. I'm speaking for him in court.
______

c I did these paintings ten years ago. It was my blue period and, as you can see, the main color in all of them is blue.
______

d We're asking a million cell phone users to answer these questions. We want to find out: are cell phones bad for us?
______

e In our laboratory we're trying to make new kinds of sunscreen.
______

f I'm arresting you on suspicion of robbery.
______

GRAMMAR 2

Review: Past Progressive

1 Underline the correct words.

I was / were waiting for you outside.

a You **was** / **were** using the computer for a long time.

b She **was** / **were** writing an email when I arrived.

c We **was** / **were** chatting online.

d Josh and Lisa **was** / **were** downloading music this morning.

e It **was** / **were** raining early this morning when I woke up.

f You and Vicki **was** / **were** playing loud music last night.

2 Write sentences using the negative and affirmative form of the past progressive.

Liam (✗ chat) online. He (✓ do) his history project.
Liam wasn't chatting online. He was doing his history project.

a I (✗ read) a blog. I (✓ watch) a video clip.

____

b He (✗ hang out) with his friends. He (✓ buy) a flash drive.

____

c They (✓ download) music. They (✗ do) their homework.

____

d We (✓ upload) pictures. We (✗ use) the scanner.

____

e You (✗ talk) on your cell phone. You (✓ take) a picture.

____

f She (✗ send) a message. She (✓ call) Josie.

____

3 Complete the questions and the answers with the past progressive form of the verbs in parentheses. Then match the questions with the answers.

a [2] Why *were you shouting* (you / shout) at the dog?

b [ ] Who __________ (make) that noise last night?

c [ ] Where __________ (you / sit) in the concert?

d [ ] What __________ (your friends / do) on the computer?

e [ ] Why __________ (Rosie / stand) in the street with her cell phone?

1 I __________ (not sit).
I __________ (stand) at the back.

2 Because he *was eating* (eat) my dinner.

3 She __________ (use) it to make a video.

4 Steve. He __________ (listen) to very loud rock music.

5 They __________ (look) at their Facebook pages.

4 Write questions using the past progressive. Then write answers for you.

What / you do / at five o'clock / on Saturday afternoon?
What were you doing at five o'clock on Saturday afternoon?
I was playing basketball in the park.

a What / you do / at ten o'clock / last night?

____

b Where / you live / five years ago?

____

c What / you wear / yesterday?

____

d What / you think about / five minutes ago?

____

e Who / you sit / next to / in the last math class?

____

GRAMMAR CHECK

1 Read the interview and circle the correct answers.

Julie Brinton tells Mark at *#Instaenglish* about her experience with an online gym.

Mark Why **a** ______ you join it?

Julie I didn't **b** ______ time to go to the gym last summer. A friend told me about an online gym and I **c** ______ to try it. First, I **d** ______ questions about my height, weight and age. Then a virtual trainer **e** ______ an exercise program for me.

Mark **f** ______ you get in shape?

Julie Yes, I **g** ______ . But there **h** ______ some problems.

Mark What kind of problems?

Julie When I **i** ______ exercises, it was often hard to see the screen. Then once, when I was lying on the floor, my cat **j** ______ on my face!

	1	2	3
a	have	did	do
b	had	has	have
c	was deciding	is deciding	decided
d	is answering	answered	was answering
e	chose	was choosing	choosed
f	Do	Were	Did
g	did	was	do
h	was	were being	were
i	was doing	did	am doing
j	jumped	jumps	was jumping

2 79 Listen and check your answers.

LISTENING

1 80 Listen to five teenagers talking about their ideal jobs. Match the letters a-e with the names.

Who …

a wants to be a scientist?

b wants to work in the music business?

c wants to work for justice in the world?

d wants to work with computers?

e wants to be a reporter?

1 ☐ Andrea

2 ☐ Joel

3 ☐ Tom

4 ☐ Mark

5 ☐ Rose

2 80 Listen again. Then write T for *true* or F for *false*.

a ☐ Andrea prefers TV to radio and newspapers.

b ☐ Joel is scared of blood.

c ☐ Mark can't act.

d ☐ Rose only wants to work in the USA.

e ☐ Tom is interested in spaceships.

EXTENSION

Circle the correct words to complete the text.

'What **a do / are** you want to be?' Why do people **b always ask / ask always** this question? My answer is always, 'I **c didn't / don't** know.' At age six, the answer **d were / was** easy for me – astronaut! Now, I **e like / liked** the idea of being a web designer. I'm **f always happy / happy always** to help friends with their computer problems. And I love **g do / doing** fun things with my computer. Yesterday, for example, I **h was / am** surfing the net when I found some great design ideas. So I scanned some old pictures. Then I **i drew / was drawing** some sketches on them with my digital pen and I **j was writing / wrote** words in a balloon coming out of someone's mouth. At the moment, I'm **k designing / design** a website for a friend. But my mom **l came / comes** into my room every ten minutes and **m says / said** helpful things like, 'Why **n are you / you are** staying inside on a lovely day like today?' So things **o is / are** going very well!

VOCABULARY PLUS

Safety Equipment

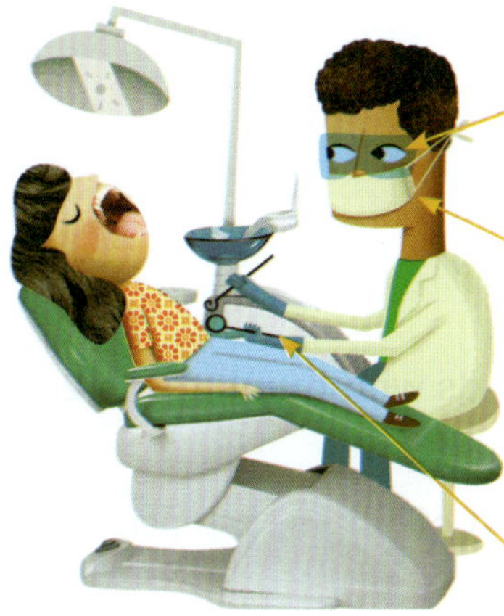

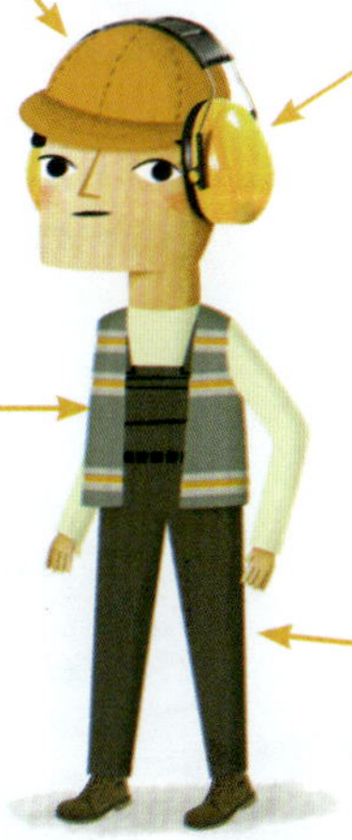

1 81 Complete the chart with the words above. Then listen and repeat.

head	eyes/ face	ears	hands	body
hat				

2 Underline the correct words.

An artist usually wears **overalls** / **a bulletproof vest**.

a A fireman usually wears **a helmet** / **ear muffs**.

b A scientist often wears **a high visibility jacket** / **safety glasses**.

c A security guard usually wears a **bulletproof vest** / **face mask**.

d A doctor often wears **disposable gloves** / **a cap**.

e A construction worker often wears a **visor** / **high visibility jacket**.

3 Read the definitions and write the words.

These are plastic and they come in pairs. *disposable gloves*

a This is made of paper and it covers your mouth. ______

b This is always a bright color like yellow or orange. ______

c This is a head covering, but it isn't hard. ______

d This is plastic and it covers your face. ______

e These are plastic and they cover your eyes. ______

2 Strange but True!

VOCABULARY 1

Prepositions

1 Match the words with numbers 1-12 in the pictures.

a [11] climb **out of**
b [ ] dive **into**
c [ ] climb **up**
d [ ] walk **along**
e [ ] sail **around**
f [ ] jump **over**
g [ ] run **towards**
h [ ] parachute **down**
i [ ] drive **away from**
j [ ] jump **through**
k [ ] swim **across**
l [ ] walk **under**

a

b

c

2 Complete the text with the prepositions in the box.

across along ~~around~~ away from
down into out of over under up

I had a strange dream last night. I was looking at a beautiful lake with an island in the middle. A boat was sailing ___around___ the island. I felt hot, so I dove **a** __________ the lake and started swimming **b** __________ it. When I got to the other side, I climbed **c** __________ the lake and lay in the sun. Then a plane flew **d** __________ me and a man parachuted **e** __________ to the grass. It was Simon. I waved at him, but he got into a car and drove **f** __________ the lake. Then I saw a river. There was a path next to the river and a bridge over the river. I started walking **g** __________ the path next to the river. I walked **h** __________ the bridge and found a mountain in front of me. My best friend was at the top of the mountain, so I wanted to run **i** __________ it, but suddenly I couldn't move. That's when I woke up.

GRAMMAR 1

Review: Simple Past and Past Progressive; *when* and *while*

1 Circle the correct words.

We were sleeping on the beach **while** / **when** somebody stole our camera.

a **While** / **When** they were cooking sausages on the beach, it started to rain.

b Where were you going **while** / **when** we met you?

c Were you watching the game **while** / **when** I called you?

d **While** / **When** I wasn't watching, she jumped out of the tree.

e We were cycling in the forest **while** / **when** we saw the bear.

2 Complete the sentences with the past progressive form of the verbs in parentheses.

I *was diving* (dive) into the lake when I hit my head.

a She fell over while she ______________ (run) to catch the bus.

b Who ______________ (you / talk) to when I saw you this morning?

c He lost his keys while he ______________ (climb) over the wall.

d ______________ (she / play) soccer when she hurt her leg?

e What ______________ (you / do) while he ______________ (make) dinner?

f ______________ (they / sit) in their living room when the thief broke the window?

3 Circle the correct words.

I **fixed** / **was fixing** my bike when Fred **sent** / **was sending** me a text.

a She **found** / **was finding** the letter from Alex while she **cleaned** / **was cleaning** her room.

b They **played** / **were playing** soccer when she **broke** / **was breaking** her leg.

c He **fell** / **was falling** out of the tree while he **picked** / **was picking** fruit.

d He **did** / **was doing** the dishes when he **cut** / **was cutting** his finger on a knife.

e While we **watched** / **were watching** TV, somebody **knocked** / **was knocking** on the door.

4 Order the words to make sentences.

living / Martin / met / were / when / Where / you / you ?

Where were you living when you met Martin?

a A bird / my breakfast / flew / having / I / into / the kitchen / was / while

____

____

b at / her bag / bus stop / a man / She / standing / stole / the / was / when

____

____

c engine trouble / flying / over / the sea / started / the / The plane / was / when

____

____

d saw / shark / swimming / the / the island / to / We / we / were / when

____

____

e getting / I / I / into / saw / snake / my tent / a / was / While

____

____

f the beach / they / some treasure / were / found / While / along / walking / they

____

____

5 Complete the sentences with the simple past or past progressive form of the verbs in parentheses.

It ___*started*___ (start) to rain while we ___*were having*___ (have) a picnic.

a I ________ (not answer) the phone because I ________ (have) my dinner.

b ________ (you / see) anything strange while you ________ (walk) by the river?

c I ________ (woke) you up because you ________ (talk) in your sleep.

d What ________ (Katrin / wear) when you ________ (see) her yesterday?

e She ________ (not hear) the bell because she ________ (listen) to very loud music.

f While she ________ (write) an email, the computer ________ (stop) working.

6 Write sentences using the past progressive or simple past form of the verbs.

While / I get / a glass of water / the cat / eat / my lunch

While I was getting a glass of water, the cat ate my lunch.

a My pet hamster / hide / in my suitcase / while / I pack / it

____

b He crash / into another car / because / he talk / on his cell phone

____

c Who drive / when / they have / the accident ?

____

d Where you sit / when / you see / the spaceship ?

____

e We dance / at a party / when / we hear / a terrible crash

____

7 Complete the text with the past progressive or simple past form of the verbs in parentheses.

Andrew Philips ___*was surfing*___ (surf) with a friend in California when a shark **a** ________ (attack) him. 'I **b** ________ (lie) on my surfboard, because I was tired, when suddenly a huge black shape **c** ________ (appear) in the water,' Andrew said. Andrew **d** ________ (shout) to his friend, Tom, but Tom **e** ________ (not understand). So Andrew **f** ________ (start) to swim very fast. 'I **g** ________ (try) not to think about the danger while I **h** ________ (swim),' he told newspaper reporters. The shark **i** ________ (bite) Andrew's arm twice. 'It **j** ________ (not hurt) very much, but there was a lot of blood and I was very frightened. Then, suddenly, six or seven dolphins **k** ________ (swim) towards me. They **l** ________ (make) a circle around me and **m** ________ (stop) the shark from getting near me. While I **n** ________ (swim) towards the shore, the dolphins **o** ________ (keep) me safe.' Andrew **p** ________ (get) very weak and tired when, luckily, Neil Turner, of the coast guard, **q** ________ (see) him.

'I **r** ________ (get) into my boat immediately and **s** ________ (go) to help him,' Neil said. 'The water around Andrew was very red because he **t** ________ (still lose) a lot of blood. I **u** ________ (lift) him out of the water immediately and **v** ________ (take) him back to the shore. When the boat **w** ________ (arrive) at the shore, a medical team **x** ________ (already wait) for Andrew. They **y** ________ (give) him first aid and **z** ________ (drive) him to hospital.

VOCABULARY 2

-ed / *-ing* Adjectives

1 Look at the pictures and complete the words.

a bor__________ c annoy__________

b bor___*ing*___ d annoy__________

e excit__________ g tir__________

f excit__________

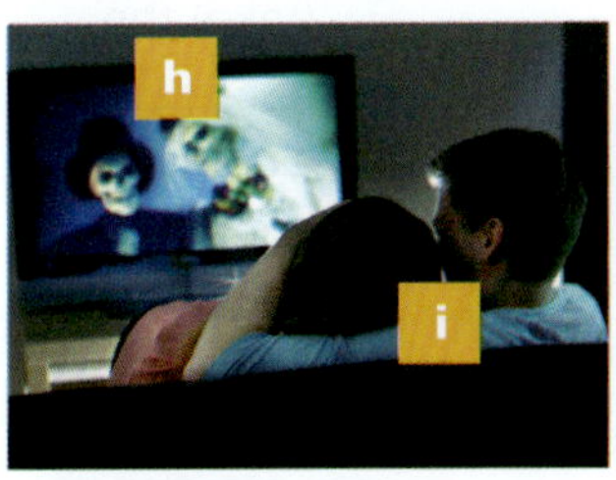

h frighten__________ j tir__________

i frighten__________

k worr__________ m interest__________

l worr__________

n surprise__________ p interest__________

o surpris__________

2 Circle the correct words.

She borrows my things and doesn't give them back. It's very **annoyed** / (**annoying**).

a He travels a lot and tells great stories. He's a very **interested** / **interesting** person.

b We're going on vacation tomorrow. I'm really **excited** / **exciting**.

c I'm very **worried** / **worrying** because I can't find my passport anywhere.

d I didn't expect to get a good grade. I was very **surprised** / **surprising**.

e The waves were really big and I'm not a good swimmer. It was **frightened** / **frightening**.

3 Complete the sentences with the words in the box.

annoyed bored boring exciting frightened frightening ~~interested~~ tired tiring

Are you __*interested*__ in birds? There's a big green one in that tree.

a Let's take the elevator to the seventh floor. Walking up the stairs is too __________.

b I got __________ with my brother last night. He was making a lot of noise and I couldn't sleep.

c I don't watch horror movies. They're too __________ for me.

d I was __________ in that class, so I started to think about the holidays.

e I'm __________ because I didn't sleep last night. I must go to bed early tonight.

f This book is very __________. I can't stop reading it.

g The bull started to run at me and I was really __________.

h The movie was really __________. I fell asleep in the middle of it.

4 Complete the sentences so they are true for you.

a I am frightened of ________________.

b I think ________________ is boring.

c When I'm annoyed, I ________________.

d I was surprised when ________________.

e I'm interested in ________________.

GRAMMAR 2

Present and Past Tenses

1 What tenses are the underlined verbs? Write *simple present, present progressive, simple past* or *past progressive*.

Why are you wearing that silly hat?
present progressive

a I always wear a hat in the sun.
____

b Did you get it in Florida?
____

c Yes, I bought it at a market.
____

d What were you doing in Florida?
____

e My parents took me there for vacation.
____

f Do you go there every year?
____

g No. We went there last year because my uncle was living there.
____

h Where's he living now?
____

i Scotland. I want to go there for New Year.
____

2 Match the sentence beginnings with the endings. Then complete the beginnings with the correct form of the verbs in parentheses.

a [3] While I *wasn't looking* (not look),
b [ ] What ____________ (you / do)
c [ ] She ____________ (drop) all the plates
d [ ] He always ____________ (wear) a suit and tie
e [ ] Look at them! They ____________ (smile)
f [ ] I ____________ (crash) the car last year
g [ ] Josie ____________ (not speak) today

1 because I was driving too fast.
2 because someone is taking their picture.
3 my little sister hid my keys under my bed.
4 when he goes to work.
5 because she has a sore throat.
6 when she heard the terrible news.
7 when you found the scorpion in your tent?

3 Complete the text with the correct form of the verbs in parentheses. Use the simple present, present progressive, simple past or past progressive.

Last summer, I *was staying* (stay) in my little house by the sea when something very strange **a** ____________ (happen). I **b** ____________ (watch) the sunset when, suddenly, a boy of about ten **c** ____________ (appear) from nowhere. He **d** ____________ (hold) a big white towel and his hair was wet. I **e** ____________ (notice) a chain around his neck with the letter 'C' on it. He said, 'My sister, Gaby, swam out to Burnt Island. Now she **f** ____________ (try) to swim back, but the current is very strong. She **g** ____________ (drown). Please do something.' I **h** ____________ (go) to my boat but the boy **i** ____________ (not come) with me. Suddenly, he wasn't there. I **j** ____________ (take) the boat towards Burnt Island and **k** ____________ (find) Gaby. She **l** ____________ (not swim) and she **m** ____________ (lie) with her face in the water. I **n** ____________ (pull) her into the boat. She was very weak, but she was alive. 'Thank you,' she said, 'I **o** ____________ (drown). You **p** ____________ (save) my life.' 'Your brother did,' I **q** ____________ (answer). 'He **r** ____________ (tell) me to help you.' Gaby **s** ____________ (start) to cry. 'I don't have a brother,' she said. 'Charlie **t** ____________ (drown) near Burnt Island last year. He was only ten years old. I **u** ____________ (think) about him every day. This was his chain. I always **v** ____________ (wear) it now.' She **w** ____________ (show) me the chain around her neck. It was the same chain as the boy's.

GRAMMAR CHECK

1 Read the text and circle the correct answers.

You probably know about hypnotists. They **a** ______ into a person's eyes and that person **b** ______ to sleep. Tanya Brooks, a talented hypnotist, and her friend **c** ______ a picnic in Yellowstone National Park when a dangerous bear came up to them. They were both so frightened, they **d** ______ away. But then, Tanya **e** ______ an excellent idea. She **f** ______ up and looked into the eyes of the bear. While she was doing this, it suddenly **g** ______ asleep. Then, Tanya and her friend **h** ______ into their car and drove away. Now, she **i** ______ a book about hypnotizing dangerous animals. But be careful! It usually **j** ______ .

	1	2	3
a	are looking	look	were looking
b	went	is going	goes
c	are having	had	were having
d	aren't running	didn't run	weren't running
e	was having	has	had
f	stood	was standing	stands
g	is falling	fell	was falling
h	were getting	did get	got
i	writes	is write	is writing
j	doesn't work	wasn't working	isn't working

2 82 Listen and check your answers.

LISTENING

1 83 Listen and number the events in the correct order.

- **a** ☐ Joss got her sweater from her bedroom.
- **b** ☐ Joss met a girl on the stairs.
- **c** ☐ Joss saw a light in her bedroom window.
- **d** ☐ Joss took a picture of a girl in her window.
- **e** ☐ Joss took some pictures of the lake.
- **f** ☐ Joss walked around the garden.
- **g** ☐ Joss went to stay with Leonie.
- **h** ☐ Joss looked for her picture of Betsy.
- **i** ☐ Leonie started practicing the piano.
- **j** ☐ Leonie told Joss about Betsy.

2 83 Listen again and circle T for *true*, F for *false* or DK for *don't know*.

- **a** There were usually a lot of visitors at Leonie's house. T / F / DK
- **b** Joss doesn't have any brothers or sisters. T / F / DK
- **c** Joss didn't know the girl on the stairs. T / F / DK
- **d** Joss was not surprised to see the light in her room. T / F / DK
- **e** The girl with the pink flower was trying to use Joss's camera. T / F / DK
- **f** Betsy was one of Leonie's cousins. T / F / DK
- **g** Joss's picture did not show Betsy. T / F / DK

EXTENSION

Underline the correct words to complete the text.

Last weekend, I **a** **was staying** / **stayed** at Gary's house in the country. Gary and I **b** **was** / **were** lying in the sun in the garden. I was trying to read a difficult philosophy book, but Gary's dog was making noise, so I **c** **didn't** / **don't** understand anything. Gary's dog loves **d** **to chase** / **chasing** after his ball, so I **e** **threw** / **was throwing** it for him. I was surprised because he **f** **didn't** / **wasn't** come back to me with it. After a bit, I **g** **was going** / **went** to look for him. He **h** **was** / **is** under a tree with a very long white bone. I got Gary to look at it. He **i** **studies** / **is studying** medicine now, so he knows about bones. Gary **j** **said** / **was saying** it's definitely a human bone. My question is: where **k** **did** / **does** the dog find it? And how and when did that person **l** **die** / **died**?

VOCABULARY PLUS

Natural Phenomena

1 ____________

2 ____________

3 ____________

4 ____________

5 ____________

6 ____________

7 ____________

8 ____________

9 ____________

10 ____________

1 84 Label the pictures with the words in the box. Then listen and repeat.

avalanche blizzard cyclone drought
hailstorm heat wave landslide
thunderstorm tsunami wildfire

2 Underline the correct words.

There is often **a drought** / **an avalanche** in hot countries in the summer.

a It was snowing and then it became a **blizzard** / **landslide**.

b The **tsunami** / **wildfire** started in the forest.

c The **drought** / **cyclone** destroyed everything in its path.

d The dark clouds were followed by a **hailstorm** / **wildfire**.

e **Thunderstorms** / **Blizzards** often occur in very hot weather.

3 Complete the definitions with the correct words.

A *tsunami* is an enormous wave in the sea.

a An ____________ is when a lot of snow moves down a mountain.

b A ____________ is an extremely strong rotating wind.

c A ____________ is when it is unusually hot for several days or weeks.

d A ____________ is when there isn't any rain for months.

e A ____________ is when a lot of earth moves down a mountain.

4 Complete these sentences for you. Try to use words from activity 1.

a In my country, there are sometimes ____________________.

b I have never seen ____________________.

c I am scared of ____________________.

3 Celebrate!

VOCABULARY 1

Clothes and Accessories

1 Order the letters and write the words. Then match them with the pictures.

[4] h t s r i -T ___*T-shirt*___

a [ ] k j e t a c ______

b [ ] s i r k t ______

c [ ] r k s n e s a e ______

d [ ] r s f a c ______

e [ ] n j s a e ______

f [ ] t s o b o ______

g [ ] t s r i h ______

h [ ] r s d e s ______

i [ ] t w s e r e a ______

j [ ] o t a c ______

k [ ] s t n p a ______

l [ ] t s s r h o ______

2 Where do the clothes go? Write the words from activity 1 in the correct group.

a on your neck ______

b on your body ______

c on your legs ______

d on your feet ______

3 Read the clues and complete the crossword.

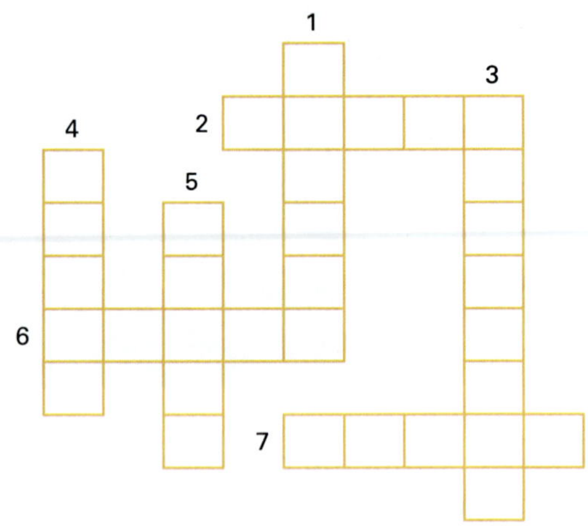

Down

1 A light coat.

3 You wear a pair of these on your feet when you're doing exercise.

4 It's only one piece and it covers your body.

5 You wear this on the top of your body. It's light and has buttons on the front.

Across

2 Jeans are an example of a pair of these.

6 Men don't usually wear this.

7 You wear this on your neck to keep warm.

4 Complete the sentences for you.

a Today I'm wearing ______.

b Yesterday I wore ______.

c On weekends I usually wear ______.

GRAMMAR 1

be going to

1 Underline the correct words.

I'm really excited. It's my brother Ned's birthday on Saturday. He **a 's / 're** going to be 18! Ned thinks we **b isn't / aren't** going to do anything special, but in fact we **c 'm / 're** going to have a big party. It **d 's / 're** going to be at home and lots of family and friends **e is / are** going to come. A DJ **f am not / isn't** going to be there, but it's OK. I **g 'm / 's** going to play music on Ned's music streaming app.

It's going to be great! ☺

2 Rewrite the sentences using the information in parentheses.

Ned's going to be unhappy on Saturday night. (happy)

Ned isn't going to be unhappy on Saturday night.

He's going to be happy.

a One thousand people are going to come to the party. (one hundred)

____

____

b Ned's going to receive two presents. (lots of)

____

____

c I'm going to wear a dress. (pants)

____

____

d The party's going to finish at 10 o'clock. (11 o'clock)

____

____

3 Complete the text with the *going to* form of the verbs in parentheses.

We have a big problem. We **a** ____________ (have) Ned's party in the garden, but the weather forecast says it **b** ____________ (rain) on Saturday evening. My parents **c** ____________ (not change) their plans. Instead, they **d** ____________ (buy) lots of umbrellas. That's silly! I **e** ____________ (tell) them to think again, but I know my dad **f** ____________ (not listen) to me. Poor Ned! The party **g** ____________ (be) a disaster in the rain! ☹

4 Look at Mark's diary and write sentences with the affirmative or negative form of *going to*.

MONDAY (today)	get up early do judo 7:00 pm
TUESDAY	no school! go to the movies
WEDNESDAY	meet Sarah – play basketball ☺
THURSDAY	buy new jeans
FRIDAY	go swimming with Leo
SATURDAY	visit grandparents
SUNDAY	

a Mark / get up early / today

____

b he / do judo / tonight

____

c he / go to school / on Tuesday

____

d Mark and Sarah / play basketball / on Wednesday

____

e Mark / buy new sneakers / on Thursday

____

f Mark and Leo / go surfing / on Friday

____

g he / visit grandparents / on the weekend

____

5 Write sentences about your future plans.

a Tonight ______________________.

b Next Thursday ______________________.

c On the weekend ______________________.

6 Complete the questions with *is* or *are*. Then match and write the answers in the box with the correct questions.

> No, he isn't. No, we aren't.
> Some soccer shoes.
> ~~Yes, I am.~~ Yes, it is. Yes, they are.

Are you going to go shopping this Saturday?
Yes, I am.

a What ___ you going to look for?
____

b ______ your dad going to drive you to the mall?
____

c ______ you and Ed going to play soccer next Sunday?
____

d ______ your parents going to buy the shoes?
____

e ______ it going to be an expensive day for them?
____

7 Order the words to make questions. Then write short answers.

going / Gemma / sunbathe / Is / to ? (✓)
Is Gemma going to sunbathe?
Yes, she is.

a swim / Are / to / going / they ? (✓)
____
____

b to / play / they / going / Are / tennis ? (✗)
____
____

c Is / rain / to / going / it ? (✓)
____
____

d cook / she / to / Is / going ? (✗)
____
____

e your dad / go / going / Is / skiing / to ? (✓)
____
____

f a coat / she / going / Is / to / wear ? (✗)
____
____

8 Complete the questions with the correct *going to* form of the verbs in parentheses. Complete the short answers.

Ted: What **a** ______________ (you / do) this Saturday night, Dad?

Dad: Your mom and I are going to go to a party at Emma's house at eight o'clock.

Ted: What type of party **b** ______________ (it / be)?

Dad: A costume party.

Ted: Really? **c** ______________ (you / buy) a costume?

Dad: No, **d** ______________. I'm going to make a cowboy costume. I'm going to wear a red shirt, boots, and a big hat.

Ted: A cowboy! **e** ______________ (Mom / go) as a cowgirl?

Dad: Yes, **f** ______________. She will wear boots, too.

Ted: **g** ______________ (all the men / go) in costumes?

Dad: Yes, **h** ______________.
i ______________ (you / see) your friends on Saturday night, Ted?

Ted: Yes, **j** ______________, but not before eight.

Dad: Why not?

Ted: Because I want to take some pictures of you – as a cowboy!

9 Answer the questions for you. Write full sentences.

a What are you going to do this weekend?
____

b Where are you going to go?
____

c Who are you going to see?
____

d What are you going to wear?
____

VOCABULARY 2

Weather and Seasons

1 Write the words in the box under the correct picture.

cloudy cold dry hot mild rainy snowy stormy sunny warm ~~wet~~ windy

wet ________________

a

____

b

____

c

____

d

____

e

____

f

____

g

____

h

____

i

____

j

____

k

____

2 Complete the sentences with the seasons in the north hemisphere.

March, April and May are in *spring*.

a December, January and February are in ________.

b September, October and November are in ________.

c June, July and August are in ________.

3 Look at the pictures and write sentences about the weather in the countries.

In Australia *it's hot and dry*.

a In France ________________.

b In Ecuador ________________.

c In Canada ________________.

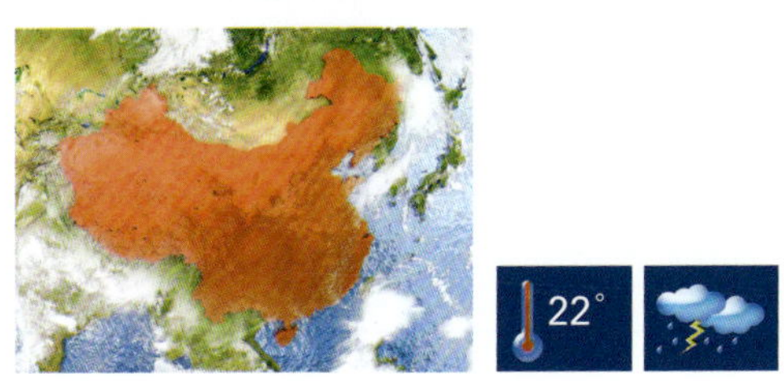

d In China ________________.

GRAMMAR 2

must / must not

1 Complete the rules with *must* or *must not.*

POOL RULES

You __must__ wear a hat.

a

You ________ eat food.

b

People ________ run.

c

You ________ swim in the correct lane.

d

You ________ listen to the lifeguard.

e

Swimmers ________ play ball games.

2 Rewrite the sentences using the pronouns in parentheses and *must* or *must not.*

Sit next to the window. (She)
She must sit next to the window.

a Don't eat in class. (You)
____

b Don't touch the video projector. (They)
____

c Listen to the teacher. (We)
____

d Do the homework again. (He)
____

e Don't wear these sneakers to school. (I)
____

3 Look at the pictures and match the beginnings a-f to the endings 1-6. Then write sentences with the phrases *You must* or *You must not.*

a	[2]	take pictures	1	on the plane
b	[ ]	drive on the left	2	in the museum
c	[ ]	talk on the phone	3	in the movie theater
d	[ ]	give any food	4	into the store
e	[ ]	take dogs	5	in Australia
f	[ ]	wear a seatbelt	6	to the animals

a

You must not take pictures in the museum.

b

____

c

____

d

____

e

____

f

____

GRAMMAR CHECK

1 Read the dialogue and circle the correct answers.

Tina Hi, Mom.
Mom Hi, Tina. What time **a** … going to be home?
Tina I'm just trying on a T-shirt and then I **b** … to come home.
Mom A T-shirt? Are you going **c** … it?
Tina Yes, **d** … . It's really cool.
Mom What color **e** … to get?
Tina Black.
Mom Black? **f** … a black one, Tina. That **g**… going to be good for summer. How about a yellow one?
Tina No, Mom. I **h** … going to buy a yellow T-shirt. I hate yellow! Look! I **i** … pay for the T-shirt so I can leave the store and go home. I have to go now. Bye!
Mom Tina? Wait a minute! Tina!

	1	2	3
a	you	you are	are you
b	'm going	'm go	going
c	buy	to buy	buys
d	am	I do	I am
e	are you going	are going you	you are going
f	Get	Don't get	Doesn't get
g	no	is aren't	isn't
h	isn't	'm not	aren't
i	must not	have not	must

2 85 Listen and check your answers.

LISTENING

1 86 Listen to the dialogue and check (✓) the picture of Phoebe. Which city is she going to visit next month?

____

☐ 

☐ 

2 86 Listen again and answer the questions.

a Who is Phoebe going to go away with?
____

b When did she go to Vancouver?
____

c Why didn't she go skiing there?
____

d What's the weather like in Aspen today?
____

e Where does Phoebe look at the weather forecast?
____

f Which clothes does Matt think she's going to need?
____

EXTENSION

Underline the correct words to complete the text.

a **You love** / **Do you love** skiing and also going to pop concerts? If the answer is *yes*, then you should go to Méribel in March next year. Why? Because b **is** / **there's** a music festival there called the *Little World Festival*. For five days c **they** / **you** can ski or snowboard during the day and then listen to some of the top DJs and pop bands at night. Méribel is a beautiful ski resort in the French Alps. d **Ago a few years** / **A few years ago**, the band The Feeling went skiing there. During their vacation, they e **played** / **'re playing** a free concert outdoors on the piste for around 6,000 people. Everyone f **was loving** / **loved** it, so the band decided to create a new annual music festival. The first Little World Festival g **was** / **were** in March 2010. I h **learn** / **'m learning** to ski right now. I i **don't go** / **'m not** skiing outdoors because it doesn't often snow where I live in the US. I can ski j **fast** / **fastly** now! I think the *Little World Festival* sounds great! I k **'m going to go** / **go** there next year with some friends.

VOCABULARY PLUS

Closet Items

1 87 Translate these words into your language. Then listen and repeat.

earrings flip-flops gloves sandals slippers sun hat tie umbrella waterproof jacket rain boots

2 Label the picture with the words from activity 1.

3 Do you wear these accessories on your feet (F), hands (H) or body (B)?

[*F*] flip-flops

a [ ] gloves
b [ ] sandals
c [ ] a tie
d [ ] waterproof jacket
e [ ] rain boots

4 Complete the sentences with words from activity 1.

When you come into the house, take off your shoes and put on your *slippers*.

a It's rainy, put on your ______ and a ______. Don't forget your ______.
b We're going to the beach. Bring your ______ for your head, and wear ______ on your feet.
c In many schools, you can't wear very long ______ in your ears.
d At weddings, the groom wears a ______ and the bride sometimes wears white ______.

5 Complete the sentences for you. Try to use words from activity 1.

a If I go to a birthday party, I'll wear ______.
b In winter, I usually wear ______.
c If it is raining, I always put on my ______.

4 Make a Difference

VOCABULARY 1

Jobs

1 Look at the pictures and complete the crossword.

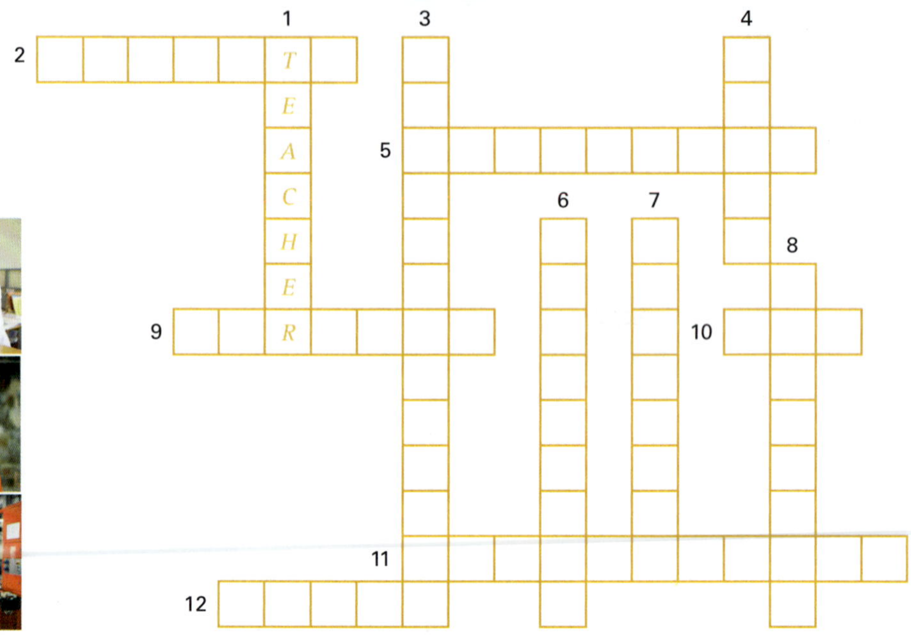

Down

Across

2 Match the words in the box with the places where the people work.

actor lifeguard mechanic
nurse ~~police officer~~ teacher

in a town center *police officer*

a at a swimming pool ______

b in a garage ______

c at a theater ______

d in a hospital ______

e in a school ______

3 Complete with words in activity 1.

a I'm looking for an interesting job that pays well. I love animals! I want to be ______.

b I'm interested in science, and how our bodies work. I can work very hard. I could be ______.

c I am interested in how things work. I like fixing things, but I don't like cars. I want to work inside. I'm going to be ______.

d I like swimming, and I'm really good at it. I want to travel and be rich! I want to be ______.

e I'm interested in design, and I'm good at art. I like looking at buildings and doing practical things. I think I'm going to be ______.

GRAMMAR 1

should (Affirmative and Negative)

1 Underline the correct words.

You **should** / **shouldn't** sleep more than five hours every night.

a Your friends **should** / **shouldn't** remember your birthday!

b You **should** / **shouldn't** eat a lot of ice cream and cake.

c You **should** / **shouldn't** drink a lot of water.

d Vets **should** / **shouldn't** like animals.

e You **should** / **shouldn't** go swimming after eating.

f Drivers **should** / **shouldn't** text while driving.

g Students **should** / **shouldn't** relax in their free time.

2 Complete the sentences with *should* or *shouldn't* and the verbs in parentheses.

She ___*should work*___ harder at school – she wants to be an architect. (work)

a You ______________ chocolate now, it's too late. (eat)

b He ______________ his teeth more often – they're black! (clean)

c We ______________ his laptop without permission. (borrow)

d You ______________ a fire outside in summer – it's dangerous. (build)

e Young children ______________ coffee. (drink)

f I ______________ my homework now before it's too late. (do)

g They ______________ in the rain (run).

3 Use the clues and *should* or *shouldn't* to create green tips.

food waste / increase
We shouldn't increase food waste.

a use / leftovers / to cook / also
____

b throw away / clothes / condition / old / good / in
____

c donate / old / repair / clothes / or
____

d bags / supermarket / buy / plastic / at
____

e our / the / bring / own / to / bags /supermarket
____

f drive / vehicles / private
____

g transportation / instead / take / public
____

4 Match the problems and recommendations to write advice sentences with *should* or *shouldn't*.

a I can't get to sleep after a long time in bed.

b I do lots of exercise and don't lose weight.

c I get too nervous before tests.

d I waste all my money on computer games.

e I'm having trouble making friends at my new school.

[ ] join a book club or a sports team

[ ] eat too much fat and sugar

[ ] spend less time at the computer

[*a*] drink some chamomile tea

[ ] study only the night before

a *You should drink some chamomile tea.*

b ______________________________

c ______________________________

d ______________________________

e ______________________________

5 Use the verbs in the box and *should* or *shouldn't* to write internet safety tips.

block	choose	download
give out	log out	respond

a You ______________ to offensive messages, even if they're from people you know.

b You ______________ attachments from someone you don't know.

c You ______________ suspicious people from your social media accounts.

d You ______________ your password to anyone except your parents.

e You ______________ from your accounts every time you finish checking them.

f You ______________ a long password to protect your accounts and devices.

6 Complete the text with *should* or *shouldn't* and the correct form of the verbs in parentheses.

Rachel
Online

Hi, Kylie,

I have a good idea for your brother's birthday! You **a** ______________ (take) him to the Kelsey Museum of Archeology in Ann Arbor. He **b** ______________ (forget) his camera. When you're in Ann Arbor you **c** ______________ (visit) the University of Michigan Museum of Natural History, too. It isn't far. You **d** ______________ (buy) a combined ticket for the two of them because it's cheaper. You **e** ______________ (visit) on Monday – the museums are closed!

See ya,

Rachel

7 Write some recommendations on how to deal with guide dogs.

a You ______________ make way for guide dogs and their owners.

b You ______________ touch or pet the guide dog while it is on duty.

c You ______________ respect the directions given by its owner at all times.

d You ______________ the guide dog without its owner's authorization.

e You ______________ the dog while it has its harness on.

f You ______________ a guide dog organization.

8 Look at Jamila's notes and write sentences with *should* or *shouldn't*.

eat pasta (✓)
drink soft drinks (✗)
go to school by car (✗)
run every morning (✓)
wear good sneakers (✓)
run near cars (✗)

She should eat pasta.

a ______________________________

b ______________________________

c ______________________________

d ______________________________

e ______________________________

VOCABULARY 2

Health Problems

1 Look at the pictures and complete the words.

a She has a c*old*__________.

b He has a c__________.

c He has a t__________.

d She has a c__________.

e She feels s__________.

2 Match a word in box A with a word in box B and write the health problems. Do you write them as one or two words?

A ~~broken~~ ear head insect sore stomach

B ache (x3) ~~arm~~ bite throat

broken arm

a ____________________

b ____________________

c ____________________

d ____________________

e ____________________

3 Look at the pictures and complete the sentences with the words in the box. Then match the sentences a-f to the responses 1-6.

broken arm cut headache insect bite sore throat stomachache

a I have a nasty __________ on my hand.

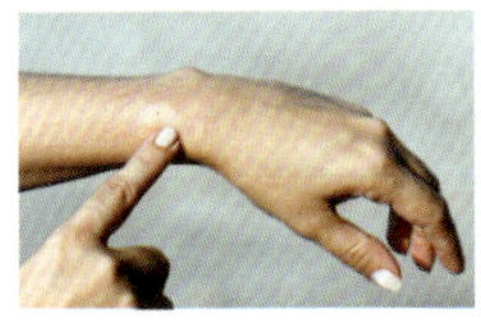

☐

b I have a __________ on my finger.

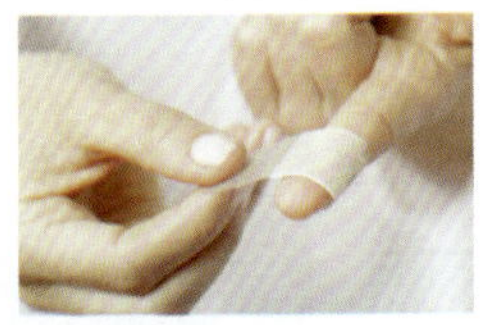

☐

c This __________ is terrible.

☐

d My __________ is getting worse.

☐

e I think I have a __________!

☐

f I have a __________ and I feel sick.

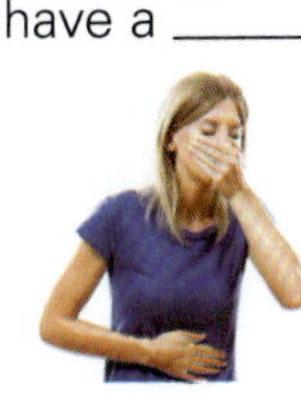

☐

1 Do you want some cough drops?

2 Come on, let's go to the hospital.

3 I think I have some special cream somewhere.

4 Put on a bandage; there are some in the bathroom.

5 Do you need an aspirin?

6 Drink some water, then lie down.

GRAMMAR 2

should (Questions and Short Answers)

1 Order the words to make questions.

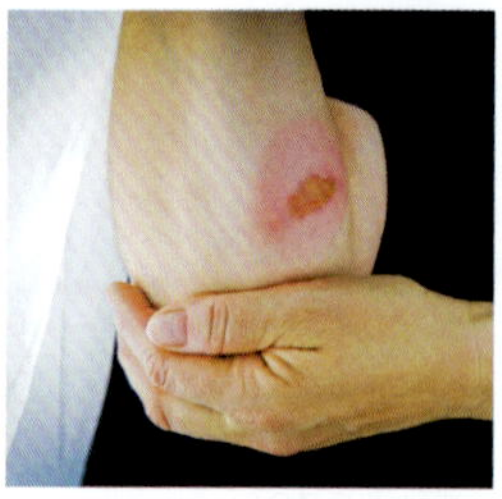

I / bandage / a / cut / Should / put / on / this ?

Should I put a bandage on this cut?

a with / us / umbrella / take / Should / we / an ?

____

b some / give / they / Should / pizza / dog / to / the ?

____

c map / a / buy / they / Should ?

____

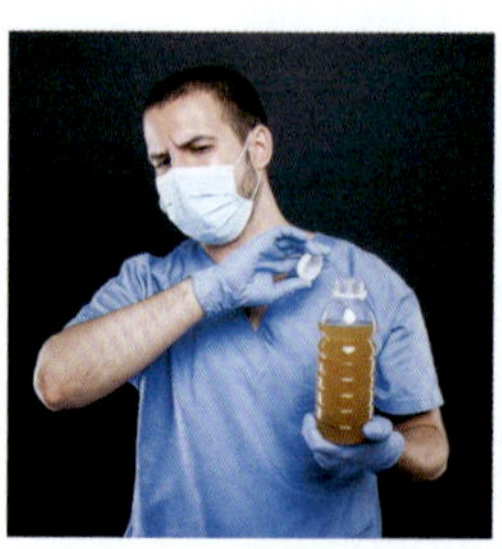

d Should / water / I / drink / the / bottle / from / this ?

____

e about / him / tell / the / Should / we / party ?

____

f Mom / Should / for / I / money / ask / some ?

____

2 Write short answers for the questions in activity 1, based on the pictures.

Yes, you should.

a ____________________

b ____________________

c ____________________

d ____________________

e ____________________

f ____________________

3 Complete the dialogue with *should* and the verbs in parentheses.

Ollie I have a test tomorrow and I can't remember anything. What **a** ______________ (I / do)?

Teacher Well, first, **b** ______________ (you / relax). **c** ______________ (you / not get) stressed – it's bad for your memory. And **d** ______________ (you / drink) water because water is good for your brain.

Ollie **e** ______________ (I / study) late at night?

Teacher No, **f** ______________! **g** ______________ (you / sleep). But the most important thing is **h** ______________ (you / not study) the night before the test. Your brain needs to rest!

GRAMMAR CHECK

1 Read the dialogue and circle the correct answers.

Liam: My mom thinks I **a** ______ study architecture when I'm older. I love architecture, but the problem is I can't draw.

Archie: You should **b** ______ some classes, then.

Liam: I'm busy with my math and science classes at the moment. I think I **c** ______ focus on these subjects first.

Archie: If you don't have time to learn to draw, **d** ______ study architecture. I think you **e** ______ think of a different profession! How about being an athlete? You're great at tennis.

Liam: No, I want to be an architect. It isn't going to be easy, but I can do it. When I'm older, I'm going to look for classes in design. They use computers – that's better for me than drawing.

Archie: You **f** ______ at school. Mr. Simms knows about courses and professions.

Liam: You **g** ______ worry so much, Archie. We're 13! Relax! Come on. Let's go and play tennis.

	1	2	3
a	shouldn't	should	should I
b	to take	take	taking
c	should	should to	shouldn't
d	should you	you aren't	you shouldn't
e	're going	should	shouldn't
f	ask	shouldn't ask	should ask
g	're going to	should	shouldn't

2 88 Listen and check your answers.

LISTENING

1 89 Listen to three telephone conversations. Circle the service each caller needs.

Caller 1: police fire ambulance

Caller 2: police fire ambulance

Caller 3: police fire ambulance

2 89 Listen again and complete the chart with information about each caller.

	Caller 1
What is the problem?	
Where is the caller?	
What should the caller do?	

	Caller 2
What is the problem?	
Where is the caller?	
What should the caller do?	

	Caller 3
What is the problem?	
Where is the caller?	
What should the caller do?	

EXTENSION

Circle the correct words to complete the text.

Médecins Sans Frontières (Doctors Without Borders, in English) is an international NGO (non-governmental organization) that supports war-ravaged countries with medical care. Founded in 1971 by a group of French doctors and journalists, MSF **a** **has helped / have helped** several nations by providing them with medicine, donations and the work of medical professionals.

Like many NGOs, MSF also needs to be supported in order to bring some comfort to people in need. What **b** **should you / you should** do to help them? First of all, you **c** **should to read / should read** as much information as possible on the MSF website, <https://www.doctorswithoutborders.org/>. You'll find detailed instructions about the various ways to contribute.

Money donation: the **d** **easiest / easier** way to support MSF is by donating money, since you can do it from anywhere in the world. One of the most important rules is that you **e** **shouldn't to / shouldn't** donate in any currency other than US dollars.

Royalty donation: an author, an actor or a musician can help by donating the royalties from their work. They **f** **should / shouldn't** contact the Fundraising Events team by telephone or email to get started.

If you **g** **can't / should** donate anything, but still think you **h** **should / shouldn't** help, you can publicize their work by sharing this information in your social media. Let's make a difference in these people's lives.

VOCABULARY PLUS

Places of Work

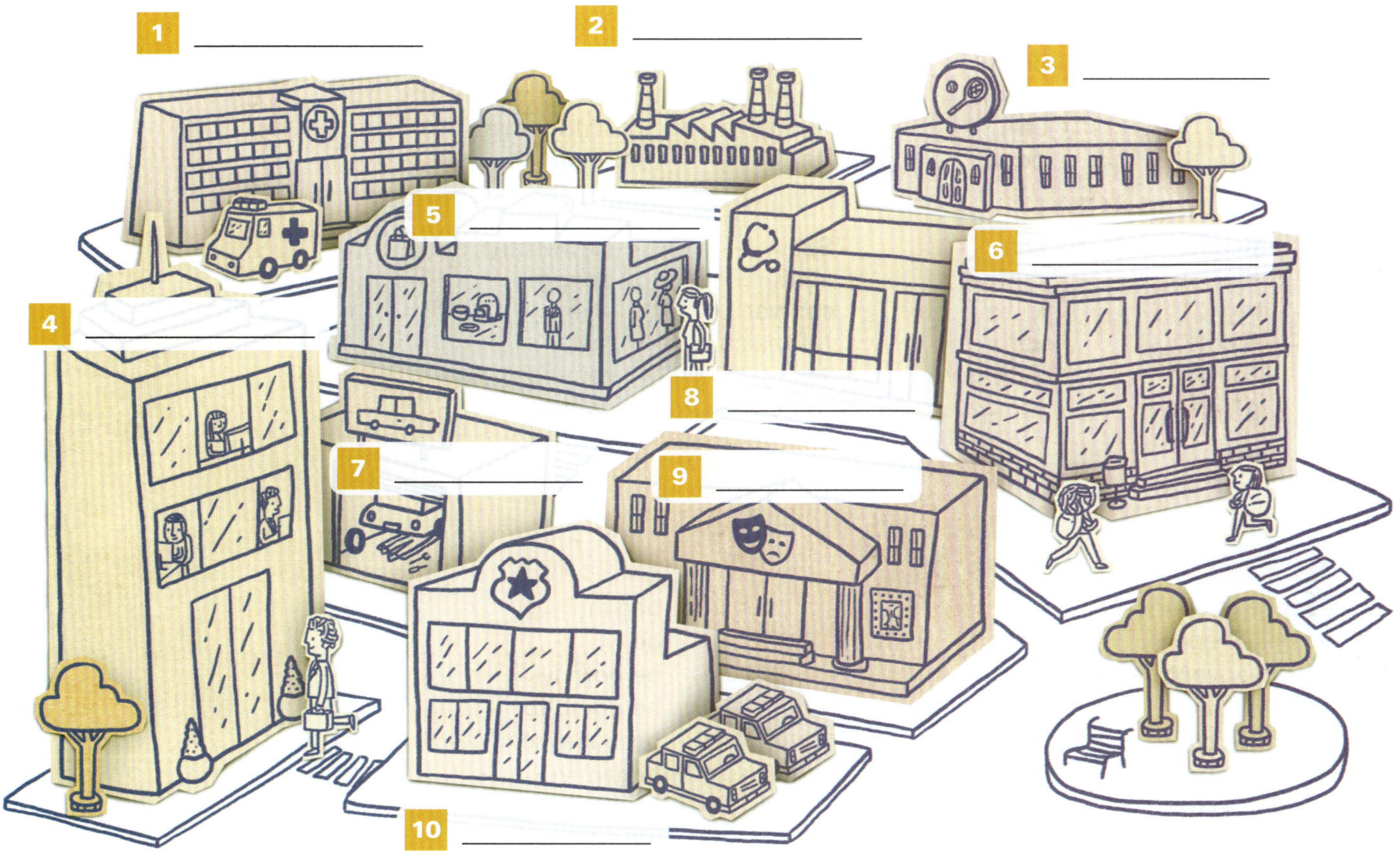

1 🔊 90 Look up the meaning of these words. Then listen and repeat.

department store doctor's office factory garage high school hospital office police station sports club theater

2 Label the picture with the words in activity 1.

3 Match the jobs a-e with the places of work 1-5.

a actor	1 high school
b police officer	2 garage
c surgeon	3 theater
d teacher	4 hospital
e mechanic	5 police station

4 Underline the correct word.

When I'm older I'm going to be a history teacher in a **high school / police station**.

a When my dog was ill, I took him to the vet's **garage / office**.

b My uncle sells computers in a very large **department store / theater**.

c My sister loves cars. She goes to our cousin's **garage / surgery** on Saturdays.

d The **office / factory** in our town makes paper.

5 Answer the questions for you. Write full sentences.

a Is there a theater in your town? Where is it?

____

b How many high schools are there in your town?

____

c How often do you go to the sports club? What do you do there?

____

Wordlist

PHONETIC CHART

VOWELS AND DIPHTHONGS 103

/ɪ/ pig	/e/ bread	/u/ lose	/aɪ/ I
/i/ she	/ɜr/ curly	/ə/ actor	/ɔɪ/ toy
/æ/ cat	/ɔ/ ball	/ʌ/ sunny	/aʊ/ mountain
/ɑ/ arm	/ʊ/ good	/eɪ/ USA	/oʊ/ boat

CONSONANTS 104

/p/ potato	/tʃ/ chair	/s/ Spain	/n/ newsstand
/b/ blue	/dʒ/ fridge	/z/ easy	/ŋ/ spring
/t/ taxi	/f/ finish	/ʃ/ shower	/l/ lake
/d/ drama	/v/ verb	/ʒ/ television	/r/ read
/k/ carrot	/θ/ bathroom	/h/ hi	/j/ yesterday
/g/ grandpa	/ð/ there	/m/ mouth	/w/ water

A 105

acoustic guitar (n) /əˈkustɪk gɪˈtɑr/
across (prep) /əˈkrɔs/
action-adventure (n) /ˈækʃ(ə)n ədˈventʃər/
actor (n) /ˈæktər/
advertise (v) /ˈædvərˌtaɪz/
advertisement (n) /ædˈvɜrtɪsmənt/
along (prep) /əˈlɔŋ/
already (adv) /ɔlˈredi/
also (adv) /ˈɔlsoʊ/
aluminum (n) /əˈlumɪnəm/
amp (n) /æmp/
anniversary (n) /ˌænɪˈvɜrs(ə)ri/
annoy (v) /əˈnɔɪ/
annoyed (adj) /əˈnɔɪd/
annoying (adj) /əˈnɔɪɪŋ/
answer (v) /ˈænsər/
apartheid (n) /əˈpɑrtˌhaɪt/
appear (v) /əˈpɪr/
architect (n) /ˈɑrkɪˌtekt/
argue (v) /ˈɑrˌgju/
argument (n) /ˈɑrgjəmənt/
around (prep) /əˈraʊnd/
artist (n) /ˈɑrtɪst/
ask (v) /æsk/
ate (v) /eɪt/
athlete (n) /ˈæθˌlit/
ATM (automated teller machine) (n) /ˌeɪ ti ˈem/
autograph (n) /ˈɔtəˌgræf/
autumn (n) /ˈɔtəm/
avalanche (n) /ˈævəˌlæntʃ/
award (n) /əˈwɔrd/
away from (prep) /əˈweɪ frɑm/

B 106

bag (n) /bæg/
be (v) /bi/
be born (v) /bi bɔrn/
be going to /bi ˈgoʊɪŋ tu/
because (conj) /bɪˈkɔz/
began (v) /bɪˈgæn/
begin (v) /bɪˈgɪn/
bill (n) /bɪl/
biomedicine (n) /ˈbaɪoʊˌmedɪsɪn/
birth (n) /bɜrθ/
birthday celebration (n) /ˈbɜrθˌdeɪ ˌseləˈbreɪʃ(ə)n/
blind (adj) /blaɪnd/
blizzard (n) /ˈblɪzərd/
boots (n) /buts/
bore (v) /bɔr/
bored (adj) /bɔrd/
boring (adj) /ˈbɔrɪŋ/
bottle (n) /ˈbɑt(ə)l/
box (n) /bɑks/
box office (n) /bɑks ˈɔfɪs/
break (v) /breɪk/
bric-a-brac sale (n) /ˈbrɪkəˌbræk seɪl/
broken arm /ˈbroʊkən ɑrm/
bulletproof vest (n) /ˈbʊlɪtˌpruf vest/
buy a house /baɪ ə haʊs/
by the end of the year /baɪ ði end əv ði jɪr/

C 107

call (v) /kɔl/
can (n) /kæn/
cardboard (n) /ˈkɑrdˌbɔrd/
carton (n) /ˈkɑrt(ə)n/
cell phone (n) /sel foʊn/
charge (v) /tʃɑrdʒ/

charge a cell phone /tʃardʒ ə sel foʊn/
chat (v) /tʃæt/
check (n) /tʃek/
chimpanzee (n) /ˌtʃɪmpæn'zi/
clean-tech (n) /klin tek/
cliff (n) /klɪf/
cloudy (adj) /'klaʊdi/
coast (n) /koʊst/
coat (n) /koʊt/
coin (n) /kɔɪn/
coin purse (n) /kɔɪn pɜrs/
cold (n) /koʊld/
collect money /kə'lekt 'mʌni/
come (v) /kʌm/
compete (v) /kəm'pit/
competition (n) /ˌkampə'tɪʃ(ə)n/
compost (v) /'kamˌpoʊst/
computer (n) /kəm'pjutər/
connect (v) /kə'nekt/
connection (n) /kə'nekʃ(ə)n/
construction worker (n) /kən'strʌkʃ(ə)n 'wɜrkər/
contaminated water (n) /kən'tæmɪˌneɪtəd 'wɔtər/
cotton (n) /'kɑt(ə)n/
cough (n) /kɑf/
cow (n) /kaʊ/
crash (v) /kræʃ/
crocodile (n) /'krɑkəˌdaɪl/
cut (v) /kʌt/
cycle (v) /'saɪk(ə)l/
cyclone (n) /'saɪˌkloʊn/

D 108

death (n) /deθ/
decorate (v) /'dekəˌreɪt/
decoration (n) /ˌdekə'reɪʃ(ə)n/
department store (n) /dɪ'pɑrtmənt stɔr/
develop (v) /dɪ'veləp/
development (n) /dɪ'veləpmənt/
die (v) /daɪ/
digital camera (n) /'dɪdʒɪt(ə)l 'kæm(ə)rə/
digital media (n) /'dɪdʒɪt(ə)l 'midiə/
director (n) /dɪ'rektər/
disease (n) /dɪ'ziz/
disposable glove (n) /dɪ'spoʊzəb(ə)l glʌv/
divorce (n) /dɪ'vɔrs/
do a sponsored swim /du ə 'spɑnsərd swɪm/
do charity work /du 'tʃerəti wɜrk/
do exercise /du 'eksərˌsaɪz/
do homework /du 'hoʊmˌwɜrk/
do nothing /du 'nʌθɪŋ/
do someone a favor /du 'sʌmwʌn ə 'feɪvər/
do your best /du jʊr best/
doctor (n) /'dɑktər/
doctor's office (n) /'dɑktərz 'ɔfɪs/
dolphin (n) /'dɑlfɪn/
dot-com company (n) /ˌdɑt'kɑm 'kʌmpəni/
down (prep) /daʊn/
download a song /'daʊnˌloʊd ə sɔŋ/
download a video clip /'daʊnˌloʊd ə 'vɪdioʊ klɪp/
dress (n) /dres/
drive (v) /draɪv/
drown (v) /draʊn/
drums (n) /drʌmz/
dry (adj) /draɪ/

E 109

earache (n) /'ɪrˌeɪk/
earmuffs (n) /'ɪrˌmʌfs/
earring (n) /'ɪrɪŋ/
educate (v) /'edʒəˌkeɪt/
education (n) /ˌedʒə'keɪʃ(ə)n/
electric bass (n) /ɪ'lektrɪk beɪs/
electric guitar (n) /ɪ'lektrɪk gɪ'tɑr/
electrician (n) /ɪˌlek'trɪʃ(ə)n/
elephant (n) /'eləfənt/
engagement (n) /ɪn'geɪdʒmənt/
engineer (n) /ˌendʒɪ'nɪr/
enjoy (v) /ɪn'dʒɔɪ/
enjoyment (n) /ɪn'dʒɔɪmənt/
equip (v) /ɪ'kwɪp/
e-reader (n) /'iridə(r)/
escape (v) /ɪ'skeɪp/
ever (adv) /'evər/
excite (v) /ɪk'saɪt/
excited (adj) /ɪk'saɪtəd/
excitement (n) /ɪk'saɪtmənt/
exciting (adj) /ɪk'saɪtɪŋ/

F 110

face mask (n) /feɪs mæsk/
factory (n) /'fækt(ə)ri/
feel (v) /fil/
fell (v) /fel/
film a scene /fɪlm ə sin/
financial service (n) /fɪ'nænʃ(ə)l 'sɜrvɪs/
fireman (n) /'faɪrmən/
flash drive (n) /flæʃ draɪv/
flew (v) /flu/
flip-flop (n) /flɪp flɑp/
flute (n) /flut/
for (prep/conj) /fɔr/
found (v) /faʊnd/
friendship (n) /'fren(d)ʃɪp/
frighten (v) /'fraɪt(ə)n/
frightened (adj) /'fraɪt(ə)nd/
frightening (adj) /'fraɪt(ə)nɪŋ/
fundraising (n) /'fʌndˌreɪzɪŋ/

G 111

games (n) /geɪms/
games console (n) /geɪms 'kɑnˌsoʊl/
garage (n) /gə'rɑʒ/
garage sale (n) /gə'rɑʒ seɪl/
get (v) /get/
get a job /get ə dʒɑb/

get married /get ˈmerid/
give (v) /gɪv/
glass (n) /glæs/
glove (n) /glʌv/
go (v) /goʊ/
go online /goʊ ˈɑnˌlaɪn/
go to /goʊ tu ˈ/
go to college /goʊ tu ˈkɑlɪdʒ/
go up /goʊ ʌp/
Good Deeds Day (n) /gʊd dids deɪ/
Goodwill Ambassador (n) /gʊdˈwɪl æmˈbæsədər/
got (v) /gɑt/
got stuck /gɑt stʌk/
grow (v) /groʊ/

H 112

hailstorm (n) /ˈheɪlˌstɔrm/
happen (v) /ˈhæpən/
have a rummage sale /hæv ə ˈrʌmɪdʒ seɪl/
have children /hæv ˈtʃɪldrən/
headache (n) /ˈhedˌeɪk/
hear (v) /hɪr/
heat wave (n) /hit weɪv/
helmet (n) /ˈhelmət/
hide (v) /haɪd/
high drama (n) /haɪ ˈdrɑmə/
high school (n) /haɪ skul/
high visibility jacket (n) /ˌhaɪ vɪzəˈbɪləti ˈdʒækət/
hold (v) /hoʊld/
Hollywood blockbuster (n) /ˈhɑliˌwʊd ˈblɑkˌbʌstər/
hospital (n) /ˈhɑspɪt(ə)l/
hot (adj) /hɑt/
how long /haʊ lɔŋ/

I 113

inform (v) /ɪnˈfɔrm/
information (n) /ˌɪnfərˈmeɪʃ(ə)n/
insect bite (n) /ˈɪnˌsekt baɪt/
inspector (n) /ɪnˈspektər/
interest (n) /ˈɪntrəst/
interested (adj) /ˈɪntrəstɪd/
interesting (adj) /ˈɪntrəstɪŋ/
internet browser (n) /ˈɪntərˌnet ˈbraʊzər/
into (prep) /ˈɪntu/
introduce (v) /ˌɪntrəˈdus/
invite (v) /ɪnˈvaɪt/

J 114

jacket (n) /ˈdʒækət/
Jamaica (n) /ʤəˈmeɪkə/
jar (n) /dʒɑr/
jeans (n) /dʒinz/
journalist (n) /ˈdʒɜrn(ə)lɪst/
just (adv) /dʒʌst/

K 115

keyboards (n) /ˈkiˌbɔrds/

L 116

lawyer (n) /ˈlɔjər/
learn to drive /lɜrn tu draɪv/
leave home /liv hoʊm/
leave school /liv skul/
leopard (n) /ˈlepərd/
lie (v) /laɪ/
lion (n) /ˈlaɪən/
listen (v) /ˈlɪs(ə)n/
live (v) /lɪv/
look (v) /lʊk/
lost (v) /lɔst/
love (v) /lʌv/

M 117

mailman (n) /ˈmeɪlˌmæn/
make (v) /meɪk/
make a charity CD /meɪk ə ˈtʃerəti ˌsi ˈdi/
make a decision /meɪk ə dɪˈsɪʒ(ə)n/
make a mistake /meɪk ə mɪˈsteɪk/
make a phone call /meɪk ə foʊn kɔl/
make friends /meɪk frendz/
make money /meɪk ˈmʌni/
make someone happy /meɪk ˈsʌmwʌn ˈhæpi/
make someone laugh /meɪk ˈsʌmwʌn læf/
manage (v) /ˈmænɪdʒ/
Maori (n) /ˈmaʊri/
market opportunity (n) /ˈmɑrkət ˌɑpərˈtunəti/
meanwhile (adv) /ˈminˌwaɪl/
mechanic (n) /məˈkænɪk/
medical field (n) /ˈmedɪk(ə)l fild/
metal (n) /ˈmet(ə)l/
mild (adj) /maɪld/
monkey (n) /ˈmʌŋki/
mountain range (n) /ˈmaʊnt(ə)n reɪndʒ/
movie premiere (n) /ˈmuvi prɪˈmir/
movie star (n) /ˈmuvi stɑr/
movie-maker (n) /ˈmuvi ˈmeɪkər/
movie-making (n) /ˈmuvi ˈmeɪkɪŋ/
multiplex movie theater (n) /ˈmʌltɪˌpleks ˈmuvi ˈθiətər/
must (v) /mʌst/

N 118

notice (v) /ˈnoʊtɪs/
nurse (n) /nɜrs/

O 119

ocean (n) /ˈoʊʃ(ə)n/
office (n) /ˈɔfɪs/
online (adj) /ˈɑnˌlaɪn/
open (v) /ˈoʊpən/
orangutan (n) /əˈræŋəˌtæn/
organize a concert /ˈɔrgəˌnaɪz ə ˈkɑnsərt/
out of (prep) /aʊt əv/
over (prep) /ˈoʊvər/
overall (n) /ˈoʊvərˌɔl/

P 120

panda (n) /ˈpændə/
paper (n) /ˈpeɪpər/
pass (v) /pæs/
pay by credit card /peɪ baɪ ˈkredɪt kɑrd/
pay in cash /peɪ ɪn kæʃ/
percussion (n) /pərˈkʌʃ(ə)n/
phone (n) /foʊn/
phone call (n) /foʊn kɔl/
phone charger (n) /foʊn ˈtʃɑrdʒər/
piano (n) /piˈænoʊ/
PIN (n) /pɪn/
play a video game /pleɪ ə ˈvɪdioʊ geɪm/
plot (n) /plɑt/
plug (v) /plʌg/
plug in a flash drive /plʌg ɪn ə flæʃ draɪv/
polar bear (n) /ˈpoʊlər ber/
police officer (n) /pəˈlis ˈɔfɪsər/
police station (n) /pəˈlis ˈsteɪʃ(ə)n/
policewoman (n) /pəˈlisˌwʊmən/
politician (n) /ˌpɑləˈtɪʃ(ə)n/
pond (n) /pɑnd/
poor sanitation (n) /pʊr ˌsænɪˈteɪʃ(ə)n/
popcorn (n) /ˈpɑpˌkɔrn/
portable hard drive (n) /ˈpɔrtəb(ə)l hɑrd draɪv/
possess (v) /pəˈzes/
possession (n) /pəˈzeʃ(ə)n/
post a comment /poʊst ə ˈkɑˌment/
predict (v) /prɪˈdɪkt/
prediction (n) /prɪˈdɪkʃ(ə)n/
prepare (v) /prɪˈper/
print a document /prɪnt ə ˈdɑkjəmənt/
producer (n) /prəˈdusər/
put (v) /pʊt/

Q 121

queue (n) /kju/

R 122

rain boot (n) /reɪn but/
rainy (adj) /ˈreɪni/
rainforest (n) /reɪnˈfɔrəst/
read an e-book /rid æn i-bʊk/
researcher (n) /rɪˈsɜrtʃər/
recognize (v) /ˈrekəgˌnaɪz/
recycle (v) /riˈsaɪk(ə)l/
reduce (v) rɪˈdus/
refer (v) /rɪˈfɜr/
release a movie /rɪˈlis ə ˈmuvi/
retirement (n) /rɪˈtaɪrmənt/
reuse (v) /ˌriˈjuz/
rhinoceros (n) /raɪˈnɑsərəs/
Royal Bengal Tiger (n) /ˈrɔɪəl ˈbeŋgəl ˈtaɪgər/

S 123

safety glasses (n) /ˈseɪfti ˈglɑsəz/
sandal (n) /ˈsænd(ə)l/
saxophone (n) /ˈsæksəˌfoʊn/
scan a picture /skæn ə ˈpɪktʃər/
scarf (n) /skɑrf/
science fiction (n) /ˈsaɪəns ˈfɪkʃ(ə)n/
scientist (n) /ˈsaɪəntɪst/
script (n) /skrɪpt/
seat (n) /sit/
see (v) /si/
sell badges /sel bædʒz/
sell candy /sel ˈkændi/
sell raffle tickets /sel ˈræf(ə)l ˈtɪkɪts/
send an email /send æn ˈiˌmeɪl/
shark attack (n) /ʃɑrk əˈtæk/
shirt (n) /ʃɜrt/
shorts (n) /ʃɔrts/
should (v) /ʃʊd/
show (v) /ʃoʊ/
sick (adj) /sɪk/
since (adv/conj/prep) /sɪns/
Singapore (n) /ˈsɪŋəˌpɔr/
skirt (n) /skɜrt/
slipper (n) /ˈslɪpər/
smart TV (n) /smɑrt ˌti ˈvi/
smile (v) /smaɪl/
snake (n) /sneɪk/
sneakers (n) /ˈsnikərz/
snowy (adj) /ˈsnoʊi/
so (adv/conj) /soʊ/
soft drink (n) /sɔft drɪŋk/
soon (adv) /sun/
sore throat (n) /sɔr θroʊt/
soundtrack (n) /ˈsaʊn(d)ˌtræk/
South Africa (n) /saʊθ ˈæfrɪkə/
special effects (n) /ˈspeʃ(ə)l ɪˈfekts/
sports club (n) /spɔrts klʌb/
spring (n) /sprɪŋ/
star in a movie /stɑr ɪn ə ˈmuvi/
start school /stɑrt skul/
stay (v) /steɪ/
stomachache (n) /ˈstʌməkeɪk/
stop (v) /stɑp/
store (v) /stɔr/
store data (n) /stɔr ˈdætə/
stormy (adj) /ˈstɔrmi/
stream (n) /strim/
study (v) /ˈstʌdi/
study abroad (n) /ˈstʌdi əˈbrɔd/
stunt (n) /stʌnt/
stunt man (n) /stʌnt mæn/
stunt woman (n) /stʌnt ˈwʊmən/
suddenly (adv) /ˈsʌd(ə)nli/
suggest (v) /səgˈdʒest/
suggestion (n) /səgˈdʒestʃ(ə)n/
summer (n) /ˈsʌmər/
sun hat (n) /sʌn hæt/
sunny (adj) /ˈsʌni/
surf (v) /sɜrf/
surf the web /sɜrf ðə web/

surgeon (n) /ˈsɜrdʒən/
surprise (v) /sərˈpraɪz/
surprised (adj) /sərˈpraɪzd/
surprising (adj) /sərˈpraɪzɪŋ/
survive (v) /sərˈvaɪv/
swam (v) /swæm/
swap meet (n) /swɑp mit/
sweater (n) /ˈswetər/
swim (v) /swɪm/

T 124

take (v) /teɪk/
take a digital picture /teɪk ə ˈdɪdʒɪt(ə)l ˈpɪktʃər/
talk (v) /tɔk/
teacher (n) /ˈtitʃər/
technician (n) /tekˈnɪʃ(ə)n/
technology sector (n) /tekˈnɑlədʒi ˈsektər/
tell (v) /tel/
temperature (n) /ˈtemp(ə)rəˌtʃʊr/
theater (n) /ˈθiətər/
then (adj/adv) /ðen/
think (v) /θɪŋk/
thunderstorm (n) /ˈθʌndərˌstɔrm/
ticket (n) /ˈtɪkɪt/
tie (n) /taɪ/
tiger (n) /ˈtaɪgər/
tip (n) /tɪp/
tire (v) /ˈtaɪr/
tired (adj) /ˈtaɪrd/
tiring (adj) /ˈtaɪrɪŋ/
tomorrow (adv) /təˈmɔroʊ/
too (adv) /tu/
took (v) /tʊk/
towards (prep) /tɔrdz/
train to be a /treɪn tu bi ə/
Trinidad and Tobago (n) /ˈtrɪnɪˌdæd ænd təˈbeɪgoʊ/
trumpet (n) /ˈtrʌmpət/
try (v) /traɪ/
T-shirt (n) /ti-ʃɜrt/
turtle (n) /ˈtɜrt(ə)l/

U 125

umbrella (n) /ʌmˈbrelə/
under (prep) /ˈʌndər/
up (prep) /ʌp/
upload (v) /ˈʌpˌloʊd/
upload a series /ˈʌpˌloʊd ə ˈsɪriz/
upload a video clip /ˈʌpˌloʊd ə ˈvɪdioʊ klɪp/
URL (n) /ˌju ɑr ˈel/
use (v) /juz/
use Instagram /juz ˈɪnstəgræm/

V 126

valley (n) /ˈvæli/
vet (n) /vet/
video clip (n) /ˈvɪdioʊ klɪp/
video game (n) /ˈvɪdioʊ geɪm/
violin (n) /ˌvaɪəˈlɪn/
visor (n) /ˈvaɪzər/

W 127

wait (v) /weɪt/
want (v) /wɑnt/
warm (adj) /wɔrm/
was (v) /wɑz/
wash cars /wɑʃ kɑrz/
water molecule (n) /ˈwɔtər ˈmɑləˌkjul/
water service (n) /ˈwɔtər ˈsɜrvɪs/
waterproof (n) /ˈwɔtərˌpruf/
waterproof jacket (n) /ˈwɔtərˌpruf ˈdʒækət/
wave (n) /weɪv/
wear (v) /wer/
web page (n) /ˈweb peɪdʒ/
website (n) /ˈwebˌsaɪt/
wedding (n) /ˈwedɪŋ/
were (v) /wɜr/
wet (adj) /wet/
while (conj) /waɪl/
wildfire (n) /ˈwaɪldˌfaɪr/
will (v) /wɪl/
win an award /wɪn æn əˈwɔrd/
windy (adj) /ˈwɪndi/
winter (n) /ˈwɪntər/
wool (n) /wʊl/
work (v) /wɜrk/
work with children /wɜrk wɪð ˈtʃɪldrən/
World Water Day (n) /wɜrld ˈwɔtər deɪ/
World Wide Web (n) /wɜrld waɪd web/
worried (adj) /ˈwʌrid/
worry (v) /ˈwʌri/
worrying (adj) /ˈwʌriɪŋ/
write (v) /raɪt/
write a blog /raɪt ə blɔg/

Y 128

yard sale (n) /jɑrd seɪl/
yet (adv) /jet/

Based on *Motivate!*
© Macmillan Publishers Limited 2013
Written by Emma Heyderman, Fiona Mauchline, Patrick Howarth, Patricia Reilly and Olivia Johnston
Grammar, *Speaking*, *Culture* and *Life Skills* pages adapted by Gisele Marçon Bastos Périgo

Director of Languages Brazil: Patricia Souza De Luccia
Publishing Manager and Field Researcher: Patricia Muradas
Content Creation Coordinator: Cristina do Vale
Art Coordinator: Jean Aranha
Content Editors: Ana Beatriz da Costa Moreira, Tatiana Martins Santana
Assistant Editors: Daniela Gonçala da Costa, Roberto Homem de Mello
Digital Editor: Bruno Lancellotti
Digital Assistant: Deborah Stafussi
Editorial Assistants: Nádia Muniz, Roberta Somera, Sheila Folgueral
Graphic Production: Alexandra L. S. Carvalho, Thais Mendes P. Galvão
Proofreaders: Paulo Winterstein, Márcia Leme, Danielle Costa
Design Concept: Martha Tadaieski
Page Make-Up: Figurattiva Editorial
Photo Research: Marcia Sato
Illustrations: Bruna Assis
Image Processing: Jean Aranha, Denis Araujo
Cover Concept: Jean Aranha
Audio: Argila Music

We would like to dedicate this book to teachers all over Brazil. We would also like to thank our clients and teachers who have helped us make this book better with their many rich contributions and feedback straight from the classroom along our long-lasting partnership!

Acknowledgments:
Adriana Dias, Adriana Leonzo, Aida Rocha de Almeida, Alessandra Andrade Nepomuceno Cirino, Alessandra Gavilan, Alessandra Marques, Alice Stela Ornelas Machado, Aline Bellarmino, Andrea Muner Paulavicius, Angela Burile Carvalho, Angela Melendez Conigliaro, Angela Segatti, Bianca Dewes, Bruno Andrade, Camila Ramalho, Cintia Galendi, Clice Pereira Salles, Clovis Viana Tavares, Cristiane Ramires, Daniela Murasaki, Danielle Pereira, Debora de Conti, Debora Thome, Eduardo Rodrigues Polidorio, Elaine Perrone, Erik Moreira, Euler França do Nascimento Júnior, Evila Rita Pinheiro Damaceno, Felipe Diesel, Fernanda Harrisberger, Fernanda Inácio, Fernanda Lucia Rocha de Sá Freire, Fernanda Maciel Machado Horta, Flavia Viana, Geraldo Vieira Júnior, Giovanna Meneguetti, Gisele Regina Dias da Silva, Glenda Rabitsch, Graciela Irene Turco, Grasiela Marques, Gustavo Rodarte Boechat, Isabella Villas-Boas, Itana Lins, Jacqueline Alves de Souza Carvalho, Juan Pablo Uribe, Juliana Gebra, Juliana Macedo Fiuza, Kelly Barboza da Silva, Kelly Cardoso, Lais Lara Maia Araújo, Leonardo Gomes de Souza, Ligia Araki, Luciana Melarato, Luciana Carnev, Malyina Kazuo, Marcela Cintra, Marcela Maria Vieira Thomazzi, Marcia Akemi, Maria Noeme de Magalhães Oliveira Monteiro, Mariani Barbosa, Michele Geledan, Milena Matos Carmona, Nair Domingues Guimarães, Patricia Salvo, Paula Bitondi, Paulo Rogério, Priscilla Rodrigues Lauro, Regina Lucia Fernandes, Renata Condi de Souza, Renata Perche, Renata Picasso Amarante, Renata Soares Cozzi Bahia, Roberta Silva, Roberta Tassinari Saraiva, Rodrigo Leão, Rôsangela Maria Silva, Samara Formagio, Sandra Magalhães, Sandra Regina Esteves Cardoso de Mello, Santo Tomaz Aquino, Sillas Paulino da Silva, Silvana Reis, Solange Ortencio, Solange Ulhoa Goulart Lucena, Soraya Bernardes da Silva, Ulysses Camargo Corrêa Diegues, Vagner Serafim, Vera Lacava.

The authors, adaptor and publishers would like to thank the following for permission to reproduce the photographic material:
p. 8: Rawpixel/iStockphoto/Getty Images, Nicolas McComber/iStockphoto/Getty Images, Verdateo/iStockphoto/Getty Images; p. 10: Ralwel/iStockphoto/Getty Images; p. 12: Prykhodov/iStockphoto/Getty Images, Adventtr/iStockphoto/Getty Images, Hocus-focus/iStockphoto/Getty Images, Adventtr/iStockphoto/Getty Images, Inspire Finder/iStockphoto/Getty Images, Scanrail/iStockphoto/Getty Images, Artisteer/iStockphoto/Getty Images, Michael Burrell/iStockphoto/Getty Images, MileA/iStockphoto/Getty Images, Lpettet/iStockphoto/Getty Images; p. 13: Sladic/iStockphoto/Getty Images; p. 14: Wsfurlan/iStockphoto/Getty Images, Goir/iStockphoto/Getty Images; p. 15: Stockcam/iStockphoto/Getty Images; p. 16: Asiseeit/iStockphoto/Getty Images, Ozgurdonmaz/iStockphoto/Getty Images, Blackzheep/iStockphoto/Getty Images, Krystiannawrocki/iStockphoto/Getty Images; p. 17: Nikada/iStockphoto/Getty Images, Imtmphoto/iStockphoto/Getty Images; p. 18: Anyaivanova/iStockphoto/Getty Images, Rob Mattingley/iStockphoto/Getty Images, Andrew Howe/iStockphoto/Getty Images, People Images/iStockphoto/Getty Images, Wdstock/iStockphoto/Getty Images, kali9/iStockphoto/Getty Images; p. 19: SWNS Picture Desk; p. 20: Pop jop/iStockphoto/Getty Images; p. 21: Onurdongel/iStockphoto/Getty Images, Hocus focus/iStockphoto/Getty Images, Pawel_p/iStockphoto/Getty Images, Monkey Business Images/iStockphoto/Getty Images, JGalione/iStockphoto/Getty Images, JazzIRT/iStockphoto/Getty Images, Ross Helen/iStockphoto/Getty Images, Lenta/iStockphoto/Getty Images, Slphotography/iStockphoto/Getty Images, Tatomm/iStockphoto/Getty Images, Fizkes/iStockphoto/Getty Images, Rawpixel/iStockphoto/Getty Images, Mario Guti/iStockphoto/Getty Images, Scyther5/iStockphoto/Getty Images, Monkey Business Images/iStockphoto/Getty Images, Pbophotographer/iStockphoto/Getty Images, Andrey Popov/iStockphoto/Getty Images, Jacoblund/iStockphoto/Getty Images, 4x6/iStockphoto/Getty Images, Gremlin/iStockphoto/Getty Images, Digtial Storm/iStockphoto/Getty Images, Aijohn784/iStockphoto/Getty Images, Yin Yang/iStockphoto/Getty Images, Steve Debenport/iStockphoto/Getty Images, Milanvirijevic/iStockphoto/Getty Images, Nomad/iStockphoto/Getty Images, Gregor Bister/iStockphoto/Getty Images, GSMsolutions; p. 24: Alatom/iStockphoto/Getty Images; p. 26: GlobalP/iStockphoto/Getty Images; p. 27: Paolo_Toffanin/iStockphoto/Getty Images, Vnarong/iStockphoto/Getty Images; p. 28: Freemixer/iStockphoto/Getty Images; p. 29: Below Surface/iStockphoto/Getty Images; p. 30: Fevre Dream/iStockphoto/Getty Images, Tramino/iStockphoto/Getty Images, Saturated/iStockphoto/Getty Images, Sturti/iStockphoto/Getty Images; p. 31: Master2/iStockphoto/Getty Images, Jeremy Richards/iStockphoto/Getty Images, Gannet77/iStockphoto/Getty Images, 0shi/iStockphoto/Getty Images, Sarosh Lodhi/iStockphoto/Getty Images; p. 35: Diego Cervo/iStockphoto/Getty Images, Btrenkel/iStockphoto/Getty Images, Web Substance/iStockphoto/Getty Images, Romolo Tavani/iStockphoto/Getty Images, G Stockstudio/iStockphoto/Getty Images, Yin Yang/iStockphoto/Getty Images, Chalabala/iStockphoto/Getty Images, People Images/iStockphoto/Getty Images, Andresr/iStockphoto/Getty Images, Wunder Visuals/iStockphoto/Getty Images, Valentin Russanov/iStockphoto/Getty Images, Extreme Photographer/iStockphoto/Getty Images, Merlas/iStockphoto/Getty Images, Martin Dimitrov/iStockphoto/Getty Images, Ferrantraite/iStockphoto/Getty Images, Cglade/iStockphoto/Getty Images; p. 38: Bjones27/iStockphoto/Getty Images, Evren Kalinbacak/iStockphoto/Getty Images, Jummie/iStockphoto/Getty Images, Sodar99/iStockphoto/Getty Images, Tim Burgess/iStockphoto/Getty Images, Seb Ra/iStockphoto/Getty Images, Jukov/iStockphoto/Getty Images, Allison Ginadaio/iStockphoto/Getty Images, Patcharin Simalhek/iStockphoto/Getty Images, Dragon Images/iStockphoto/Getty Images, BraunS/iStockphoto/Getty Images, Mladen Kostic/iStockphoto/Getty Images, Katarzyna Bialasiewicz/iStockphoto/Getty Images, Alex Brylov/iStockphoto/Getty Images, Martin dm/iStockphoto/Getty Images, Adventtr/iStockphoto/Getty Images, Gilaxia/iStockphoto/Getty Images, pro6x7/iStockphoto/Getty Images, nd3000/iStockphoto/Getty Images, Tarik Kizilkaya/iStockphoto/Getty Images; p. 42: Wundervisuals/iStockphoto/Getty Images; p. 44: Shapecharge/iStockphoto/Getty Images dolgachov/iStockphoto/Getty

Images, GlobalStock/iStockphoto/Getty Images, LightField Studios/iStockphoto/Getty Images, Sarah Kate Dorman/iStockphoto/Getty Images, Mohammed Elshamy/Anadolu Agency/Getty Images; p. 46: bugsmom/iStockphoto/Getty Images; p. 48: FatCamera/iStockphoto/Getty Images, Tarasov_vl/iStockphoto/Getty Images, Thiago Santos/iStockphoto/Getty Images; p. 49: Pawel Gaul/iStockphoto/Getty Images, BraunS/iStockphoto/Getty Images, Vince Talotta/Toronto Star/Getty Images; p. 50: Rike/iStockphoto/Getty Images, Grafner/iStockphoto/Getty Images,Vit-plus/iStockphoto/Getty Images, Smitt/iStockphoto/Getty Images; p. 51: Theo Wargo/Getty Images; p. 52: Akg Images/Fotoarena, Nubephoto/iStockphoto/Getty Images; p. 53: Iryna_L/iStockphoto/Getty Images, Bonetta/iStockphoto/Getty Images, Tarzhanova/iStockphoto/Getty Images, Poplasen/iStockphoto/Getty Images, Venakr/iStockphoto/Getty Images, Bettina Sentner/iStockphoto/Getty Images, Rolleiflextlr/iStockphoto/Getty Images, Domin domin/iStockphoto/Getty Images, Tarzhanova/iStockphoto/Getty Images, TPopova/iStockphoto/Getty Images GoodLifeStudio/iStockphoto/Getty Images, Studiocasper/iStockphoto/Getty Images, Simonbradfield/iStockphoto/Getty Images, AlinaMD/iStockphoto/Getty Images, Denis TangneyJr/iStockphoto/Getty Images, Andrew Mayovskyy/iStockphoto/Getty Images, Jctabb/iStockphoto/Getty Images, AGrigorjeva/iStockphoto/Getty Images, Kavram/iStockphoto/Getty Images, aetb/iStockphoto/Getty Images, Cinoby/iStockphoto/Getty Images, Marian Vejcik/iStockphoto/Getty Images, Willowpix/iStockphoto/Getty Images, Dreef/iStockphoto/Getty Images, AGrigorjeva/iStockphoto/Getty Images, CrazyD/iStockphoto/Getty Images, Jimmy villalta/iStockphoto/Getty Images, Bulgac/iStockphoto/Getty Images, Ctermit/iStockphoto/Getty Images; p. 56: kertlis/iStockphoto/Getty Images; p. 58: Squared pixels/iStockphoto/Getty Images, Wavebreakmedia/iStockphoto/Getty Images, Michael Jung/iStockphoto/Getty Images; p. 59: Fat Camera/iStockphoto/Getty Images, Uncleroo/iStockphoto/Getty Images, Gchutka/iStockphoto/Getty Images, Ruben Sprich/Reuters/Fotoarena; p. 60: Christopher Bernard/iStockphoto/Getty Images; p. 61: MarKord/iStockphoto/Getty Images, Weerapatkia tdumrong/iStockphoto/Getty Images, Pablo Rodriguez1/iStockphoto/Getty Images, Phil Augustavo/iStockphoto/Getty Images, Justhavealook/iStockphoto/Getty Images, SelectStock/iStockphoto/Getty Images, Alamy/Fotoarena; p. 62: Chatchaisura kram/iStockphoto/Getty Images, Olga Belova/iStockphoto/Getty Images, Subtropica/iStockphoto/Getty Images, Filo/iStockphoto/Getty Images; p. 63: Pabst Ell/iStockphoto/Getty Images, Pavalena/iStockphoto/Getty Images; p. 64: Baiajaku/iStockphoto/Getty Images; p. 65: dorioconnell/iStockphoto/Getty Images; p. 66: Monkeybusinessimages/iStockphoto/Getty Images, XiXinXing/iStockphoto/Getty Images; p. 67: Joegolby/iStockphoto/Getty Images, Yacobchuk/iStockphoto/Getty Images, Lovro77/iStockphoto/Getty Images, Evgeniy Shkolenko/iStockphoto/Getty Images, Vale_t/iStockphoto/Getty Images, Sturti/iStockphoto/Getty Images, Wave breakmedia/iStockphoto/Getty Images, Gauthier2902/iStockphoto/Getty Images, Andresr/iStockphoto/Getty Images, Muratkoc/iStockphoto/Getty Images, Steve Debenport/iStockphoto/Getty Images, Jevtic/iStockphoto/Getty Images, p. 69: Gilaxia/iStockphoto/Getty Images, Images by barbara/iStockphoto/Getty Images, M-gucci/iStockphoto/Getty Images, Johnny Greig/iStockphoto/Getty Images, Semata design/iStockphoto/Getty Images, Wavebreakmedia/iStockphoto/Getty Images; p. 70: Shironosov/iStockphoto/Getty Images, Xijian/iStockphoto/Getty Images, Karammiri/iStockphoto/Getty Images, Nys444/iStockphoto/Getty Images, Wavebreakmedia/iStockphoto/Getty Images, Rusm/iStockphoto/Getty Images, Laflor/iStockphoto/Getty Images, Baona/iStockphoto/Getty Images, Ben Gingell/iStockphoto/Getty Images, Casarsa/iStockphoto/Getty Images, Simplytheyu/iStockphoto/Getty Images, Skynesher/iStockphoto/Getty Images, Gchutka/iStockphoto/Getty Images; p. 73: Filadendron/iStockphoto/Getty Images; p. 74: Martin-dm/iStockphoto/Getty Images, Rvlsoft/iStockphoto/Getty Images; p. 75: Tzido/iStockphoto/Getty Images, Mmartboy10/iStockphoto/Getty Images; p. 144: Meilun/iStockphoto/Getty Images; p. 145: AlfazetChronicles/iStockphoto/Getty Images; p. 146: Bombuscreative/iStockphoto/Getty Images, Ronstik/iStockphoto/Getty Images, Juststock/iStockphoto/Getty Images, Hocus-focus/iStockphoto/Getty Images, People Images/iStockphoto/Getty Images, Mikkel william/iStockphoto/Getty Images; p. 147: Believe In Me/iStockphoto/Getty Images; p. 149: Aquariagirl1970/iStockphoto/Getty Images, Bill Oxford/iStockphoto/Getty Images, Fullvalue/iStockphoto/Getty Images, Sunara/iStockphoto/Getty Images, Gkrphoto/iStockphoto/Getty Images, Artisteer/iStockphoto/Getty Images, Plain View/iStockphoto/Getty Images, Shansekala/iStockphoto/Getty Images; p. 151: Antonio Guillem/iStockphoto/Getty Images, Rawpixel/iStockphoto/Getty Images; p. 152: Mixetto/iStockphoto/Getty Images, Sashatigar/iStockphoto/Getty Images; p. 155: Olaf Speier/iStockphoto/Getty Images; p. 157: Martin Dim/iStockphoto/Getty Images, Dmytro Aksonov/iStockphoto/Getty Images, Yin Yang/iStockphoto/Getty Images, Sturti/iStockphoto/Getty Images, Urosh Petrovic/iStockphoto/Getty Images, FatCamera/iStockphoto/Getty Images, Gibson Pictures/iStockphoto/Getty Images, Amygdala Imagery/iStockphoto/Getty Images, Stock Colors/iStockphoto/Getty Images,Drazen/iStockphoto/Getty Images; p. 159: zomby007/iStockphoto/Getty Images; p. 161: Lysogor/iStockphoto/Getty Images, Kovshutin Denis/iStockphoto/Getty Images, Ig0rZh/iStockphoto/Getty Images, Pgiam/iStockphoto/Getty Images, Eddtoro/iStockphoto/Getty Images, TAGSTOCK1/iStockphoto/Getty Images, NASA Goddard, Cinoby/iStockphoto/Getty Images, Mdesigner125/iStockphoto/Getty Images, Mac99/iStockphoto/Getty Images; p. 162: Tarzhanova/iStockphoto/Getty Images, Sankai/iStockphoto/Getty Images, Heinteh/iStockphoto/Getty Images, Mawielobob/iStockphoto/Getty Images, Tarzhanova/iStockphoto/Getty Images, Mawielobob/iStockphoto/Getty Images, Media Production/iStockphoto/Getty Images, Tarzhanova/iStockphoto/Getty Images, Domin_domin/iStockphoto/Getty Images, Siraphol/iStockphoto/Getty Images, Flyfloor/iStockphoto/Getty Images, Rolleiflextlr/iStockphoto/Getty Images; p. 163: Vesna Andjic/iStockphoto/Getty Images; p. 165: Pawel Gaul/iStockphoto/Getty Images, Rapid Eye/iStockphoto/Getty Images, Sadeugra/iStockphoto/Getty Images, Marccophoto/iStockphoto/Getty Images,Tcsaba/iStockphoto/Getty Images, Marian Vejcik/iStockphoto/Getty Images, Andrey Danilovich/iStockphoto/Getty Images, Robertiez/iStockphoto/Getty Images, Pixdeluxe/iStockphoto/Getty Images, Jctabb/iStockphoto/Getty Images, Snpolus/iStockphoto/Getty Images, Mammuth/iStockphoto/Getty Images, Da photos/iStockphoto/Getty Images, Harvepino/iStockphoto/Getty Images; p. 168: Adventure Photo/iStockphoto/Getty Images; p. 170: Gradyreese/iStockphoto/Getty Images, Aijohn784/iStockphoto/Getty Images, Steve Debenport/iStockphoto/Getty Images, Monkeybusinessimages/iStockphoto/Getty Images, Martinan/iStockphoto/Getty Images, M_a_y_a/iStockphoto/Getty Images, Fang Xia Nuo/iStockphoto/Getty Images, Gchutka/iStockphoto/Getty Images, Kupicoo/iStockphoto/Getty Images, JackF/iStockphoto/Getty Images, Shinyfamily/iStockphoto/Getty Images, Diego Cervo/iStockphoto/Getty Images; p. 171: Tatiana Dyuvbanova/iStockphoto/Getty Images; p. 172: Bobbymn/iStockphoto/Getty Images, Ruslan Dashinsky/iStockphoto/Getty Images; p. 173: Steve Debenport/iStockphoto/Getty Images, Saiyood/iStockphoto/Getty Images, Image Source/iStockphoto/Getty Images, kwanchai chaiudom/iStockphoto/Getty Images, Eyenigelen/iStockphoto/Getty Images, HAYKIRDI/iStockphoto/Getty Images, Temmuzcan/iStockphoto/Getty Images, kimberrywood/iStockphoto/Getty Images, 9nong/iStockphoto/Getty Images, M Master1305/iStockphoto/Getty Images, LittleBee80/iStockphoto/Getty Images; p. 174: Positive Focus/iStockphoto/Getty Images, Jure/iStockphoto/Getty Images, Anchiy/iStockphoto/Getty Images, Praetorian photo/iStockphoto/Getty Images, Catalin205/iStockphoto/Getty Images, Katarzyna Bialasiewicz/iStockphoto/Getty Images, Azman/iStockphoto/Getty Images, Monkey business images/iStockphoto/Getty Images; p. 175: Monkey business images/iStockphoto/Getty Images, M_a_y_a/iStockphoto/Getty Images; p. 176: Laflor/iStockphoto/Getty Images.

Dados Internacionais de Catalogação na Publicação (CIP)

H531i Heyderman, Emma
1.ed. InstaEnglish Student's Book & Workbook 2: Split A / Emma Heyderman... [et al.]. – 1.ed. – São Paulo: Macmillan Education do Brasil, 2020.
120 p.; il.; 21 x 29,7 cm.

ISBN: 978-65-5752-000-0

1. Língua inglesa. I. Mauchline, Fiona. II. Howarth, Patrick. III. Reilly, Patricia. IV. Johnston, Olivia. V. Título.

CDD 420
04-2020/3 CDU 811.111

Índice para catálogo sistemático:

1. Língua inglesa

Bibliotecária responsável: Aline Graziele Benitez CRB-1/3129

MACMILLAN EDUCATION DO BRASIL
Av. Brigadeiro Faria Lima, 1.309, 3° Andar –
Jd. Paulistano – São Paulo – SP – 01452-002
www.macmillan.com.br
Customer Service: [55] (11) 4613-2278
0800 16 88 77
Fax: [55] (11) 4612-6098

Printed in Brazil. First print. April, 2020.

NOTES

NOTES